THE FOL

POCK

to

COLLECTABLE CAMERAS

and other

PHOTOGRAPHICA

Martin Russell & Ron Lockton

Also by Martin Russell and Ron Lockton

A Price Guide to Collectable Cameras published 1983
reprinted 1984

The Fountain Press Price Guide to Collectable Cameras
published 1986

Fountain Press Ltd
45 The Broadway
Tolworth
Surrey KT6 7DW
England

ISBN 0 86343 001 5

Printed and Bound in Great Britain
by Short Run Press Ltd.

PREFACE

The most frequent comments on our "Price Guides to Collectable Cameras" have been that they should contain price information on many more items and be sized to be a constant companion at shows, fairs or auctions.

Hence the "Pocket Price Guide to Collectable Cameras" which complements the main edition. As before the principal data source is the regular auctions of Photographica held by Christie's which ensures an objective and independent supply of up-to-date internationally recognised prices covering a wide range of photographica.

However many of the lower value, but nontheless very collectable cameras and other items of photographica, do not come up for auction at Christie's as "singleton" lots. Therefore our data basis has been widened to include the prices realised at the quarterly postal auctions held by the Photographic Collectors Club of Great Britain (PCC GB).

In these auctions items are bid for against a known reserve and do not attract a buyers premium. As general rule the prices realised tend to be slightly lower than those at Christie's for the, infrequent occurring, comparable items.

We should like to take this opportunity of expressing our thanks, both to the Photogaphic Collectors Club of Great Britain and to Christie' South Kensington Ltd for their cooperation in producing this Guide.

Our thanks also to members of the PCC GB for their help and assistance in its preparation either by contributing to the text or the illustrations. In particular we should like to thank Mike Rees, and Stein Falchenberg for their comments and advice.

NOTES on USING the GUIDE

An item can be found by using the INDEX which lists all titles in alphabetical order by reference number and page.

Items in the Price Data pages are listed in alphabetical order by MAKER except for the last section which is headed VARIOUS MAKERS and gives prices of generalised types of cameras and other photographica. This section should be be used to estimate the prices of items not covered individually or whose maker is not known.

Makers Names are in capitals throughout, and one heading is used to include name changes and manufacturers amalgamations (e.g. HOUGHTON includes H.B.M.) Where an item was sold by both a pre-amalgamation and a post-amalgamation maker (e.g. 'Ideal' by both ICA and ZEISS IKON) and the auction prices are very similar then a common heading (e.g. ICA/ZEISS IKON) may be used.
(See note on page 113 re manufacturers names.)

The Reference Number is unique to the item and comprises a letter P,Q,R,S, or T, and a number. The letter classifies an item as being in one of the following groups:-

P - Plate cameras. R - Rollfilm cameras.
Q - 35mm cameras. S - Sub-miniature cameras & other items.
T - Leitz cameras, lenses and other items.

Items are listed alphabetically and numerically after each of these letters. The symbol > before the Ref. No. indicates that the item is illustrated with notes on the facing page.

Titles are either the items name (in quotes ' ') or the descriptive type. Some titles have been shortened or modified to assist in easier cataloguing. Information on format or features etc is included after the title to help identification.

Many categories cover common variants and sizes of a basic type of camera or cameras as, contrary to expectations perhaps, in many cases variations have little effect on auction prices. Where they do they are treated as separate items. Some unusual variants of interest to specialist collectors are not distinguished in auction catalogue descriptions or this Guide.

The data columns show the source and quality of the base data used in compiling the prices. Each Christie based item is "starred"(*) and has a rating according to the number of usable auction appearances during the past five years or so.

* - Price is based on a single auction and is therefore only indicative of its likely value.

** - Has appeared up to four times and the price is the weighted average of the realised prices.

*** and **** - Have appeared up to eight or sixteen times respectively, whilst ***** items have appeared up to thirty two or more times. Prices of these items are statistically calculated.

Guide Prices are given in £ sterling and U.S. $ using an exchange rate of 1.75$ to the £.

For PCC items the price band shown is that into which all, or the majority, of the prices realised have fallen.

For Christie auction items the price range shown is that into which an average condition item can be expected to fall. Note that since mid-1986 the Christie prices have included a 10% buyers premium, which is included in our base data.

Average condition is not easily defined and varies according to the type, age and rarity of the item considered. As a rough definition one would expect an average item to be in good working order, not badly marked, and unmodified. From this basis mint condition items could attract a premium of 75 to 100%, whilst one fit only for restoration and repair a reduction of 50 to 75%.

Between these limits is the area for judgement, bargaining, etc. The Price Range gives a reasonable starting point for these negotiations, which will be viewed differently by a buyer or seller!

Abbreviations used in addition to the conventional ones are:-

a. - rounded approximate price.

lots - items auctioned in quantity.

outfit - a camera and accessories (often in a fitted case), and having a price substantially greater than the camera alone.

? - after an item, that the authenticity of its make is in some doubt.

Ref	Name	Data	Average Condition Price Range £	$
A&N AUXILIARY C.S. (London)				
P1	Tailboard 1/2 plate	**	80-100	140-170
ABRAHAM R (London)				
P2	Tailboard 1/2 plate	*	a. 80	a. 140
ADAMS A. (London)				
P3	'Adams de Luxe' 1/4 pl H & S	**	260-320	460-550
> P4	'Aidex' folding S.L.R. 1/4 pl	*	a. 260	a. 460
P5	Hand with changing box 1/4 pl	*	a. 100	a. 180
P6	'Hand Practical' 1/1 plate	*	a. 110	a. 190
P7	'Idento' strut camera	***	80-100	140-170
P8	'Minex' S.L.R. 2 1/4 * 3 1/4	**	140-170	240-300
P9	'Minex' S.L.R. 1/4 plate	**	90-110	160-200
P10	'Minex' S.L.R. trop. 1/4 pl	**	3500-4300	6200-7600
P11	'Royal' field 1/4 plate	*	a. 75	a. 130
P12	'Vaido' Hand & Stand 5 * 4 in	*	a. 160	a. 280
> P13	'Vesta' folding	***	65-80	110-140
P14	'Vesta' outfit	*	a. 160	a. 280
P15	'Videx' S.L.R.	***	55-65	95-120
P16	'Yale' magazine 5 * 4 in.	*	a. 40	a. 70
ADAMS R.T (England)				
P17	Tailboard 1/1 plate	**	80-100	140-170
ADOX (Wiesbaden) see also Q237 page 106				
Q1	'Adox 300' (magazine back)	*	a. 80	a. 140
R1	'Golf' folding 6 * 6 cm.	pcc	8-15	13-25
A.F.I.O.M. (Italy)				
Q2	'Kristall' (Leica copy)	*	a. 20	a. 35
AGFA (Munich)				
Q3	'Ambiflex 11' S.L.R.	pcc	20-40	35-70
Q4	'Colorflex' S.L.R.	**	30-35	50-60
> Q5	'Flexilette' T.L.R.	***	35-45	65-80
Q6	'Karat' (early type)	pcc	15-30	25-50
Q7	'Karat' (most pre-war)	pcc	8-15	13-25
Q8	'Karat' (post-war) c.r.f	pcc	20-40	35-70
Q9	'Optima' T.L.R.	*	a. 30	a. 55
Q10	'Optima' (most models)	pcc	5-10	9-18
Q11	'Optima 335 Sensor'	pcc	15-30	25-50

> P4. 'Aidex' 1/4 plate
... This elegant camera was the last ADAMS version of the folding S.L.R. It had a self-capping focal plane shutter and a lens panel held rigid by struts in the same manner as the 'Vesta' folding camera P13 below. Also made in 3 1/2 * 2 1/2 in. size. c.1928

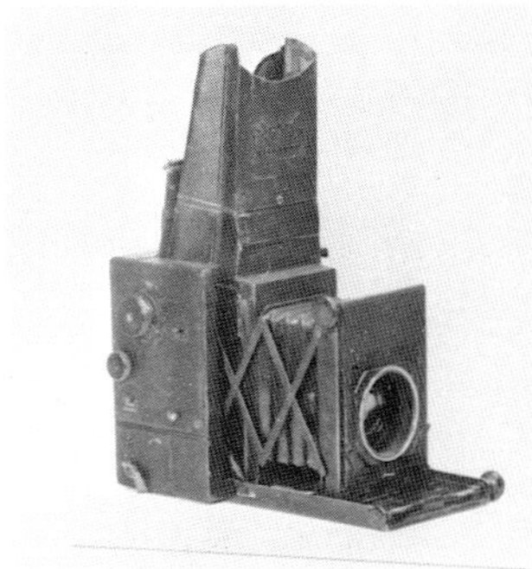

> P13. 'Vesta'
... A folding plate camera made from c.1892 in several sizes. The lens panel is held rigid by a trellis of lazy tongs as the panel is pulled out to the infinity position. The model shown (c.1912) has a focal plane shutter which is an uncommon feature in folding cameras.

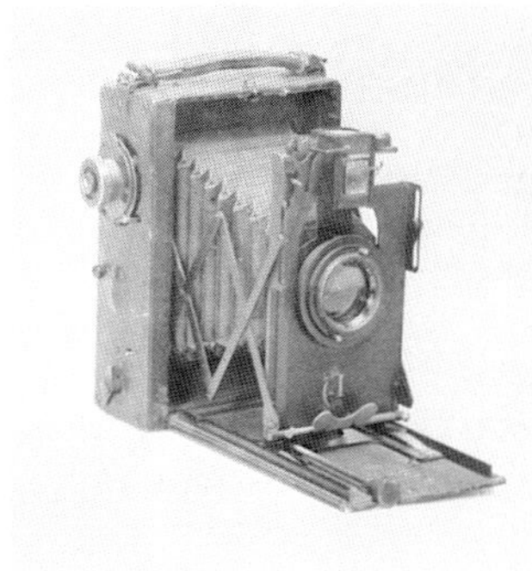

> Q5. 'Flexilette' T.L.R.
... A 35 mm. T.L.R. c.1960 The taking (f2.8 45mm. Apotar) and viewing lenses were placed very close together in a common focussing mount to virtually eliminate parallax errors down to the minimum focussing distance of three feet.

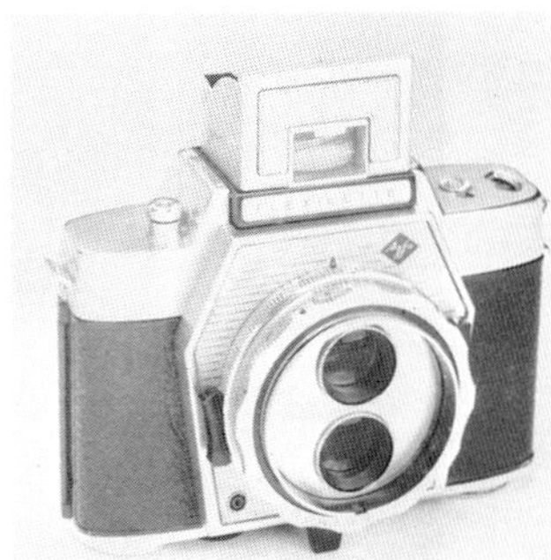

AGFA (Munich)(cont'd)

Ref	Name	Data	Average Condition Price Range £	$
> Q12	'Silette' (simple models)	pcc	5-10	9-18
Q13	'Solinette' folding	**	14-17	25-30
Q14	'Super Silette' (Solinar f3.5)	pcc	8-15	13-25
Q15	'Super Silette' (Solagon f2)	pcc	20-40	35-70
R2	'Billy' (Record etc)	pcc	8-15	13-25
R3	'Clack' (8 on 120) box	pcc	5-10	9-18
R4	Folding hide covered	*	a. 30	a. 55
R5	Folding V.P.	**	25-30	45-55
R6	'Isolette 1' folding	pcc	5-10	9-18
R7	'Isolette 11' folding	pcc	15-30	25-50
R8	'Isolette Super' c.r.f.	**	60-75	110-130
R9	'Speedex' folding	pcc	8-15	13-25
R10	'Standard' folding	**	17-20	30-35
R11	'Synchro-Box' art-deco	pcc	Under 5	Under 9
AGFA/ANSCO (New York)				
Q16	'Memo' (half frame)	***	50-60	85-100
Q17	'Memo' (full frame)	*	a. 20	a. 35
Q18	'Memo 11' (spring motor auto)	**	16-20	30-35
R12	'Automatic 1A' (motor driven)	**	80-100	140-170
R13	'Bionic' folding	*	a. 12	a. 20
R14	'Clipper' (16 on 116)	pcc	5-10	9-18
R15	'G.P. Recording Camera No 19'	*	a. 30	a. 55
R16	'Readyset' folding	**	18-20	30-35
A.G.I. (Croydon England)				
Q19	'Agimatic' (uncoupled r.f.)	pcc	8-15	13-25
R17	'Agiflex' S.L.R.	**	50-60	85-100
> R18	'Agifold' (uncoupled r.f.)	pcc	8-15	13-25
R19	'Agilux Super 44'	pcc	8-15	13-25
AIRES (Tokyo)				
Q20	'Aires 35' S.L.R.	pcc	15-30	25-50
AMERICAN CAMERA (London)				
> S1	'Demon Detective'	***	550-650	950-1200
AMERICAN MINUTE PHOTO (Chicago)				
S2	Tintype camera	*	a. 75	a. 130
AMERICAN RAND (New York)				
R20	'Photo Binocular' (telephoto)	*	a. 45	a. 80

> Q12 'Silette' models

... This category covers the simpler models in the range without built-in exposure meter or rangefinder.
Lenses fitted were the 45mm f3.5 Apotar or f2.8 Color Agnar in one of the Pronto range of shutters. Introduced 1954 the Silette range was extensive and varied.

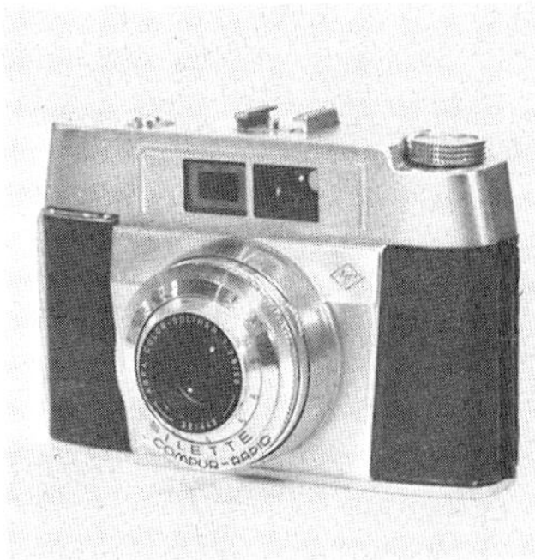

> R18. 'Agifold'

... The standard Agifold C.1949 was a 2 1/4 sq. folder for 120 or 620 film with f4.5 Agilux lens in a 4 or 8 speed shutter. The 1950 version incorporated an uncoupled rangefinder with an optical viewfinder. It also had a variable density optical exposure meter.

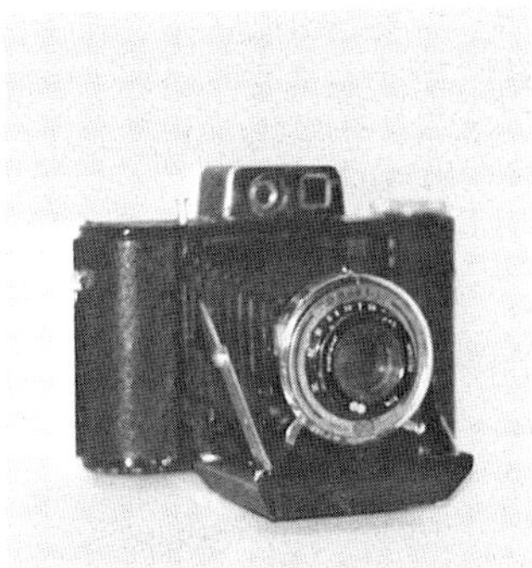

> S1. 'Demon Detective'

... An unusual camera designed by a Mr. O'Reilly for the AMERICAN CAMERA Co. in London having a shutter powered by an elastic band. Its nicest feature-its back-was engraved 'The Wonder of the World'. If you believed that you would believe anything! c.1889.

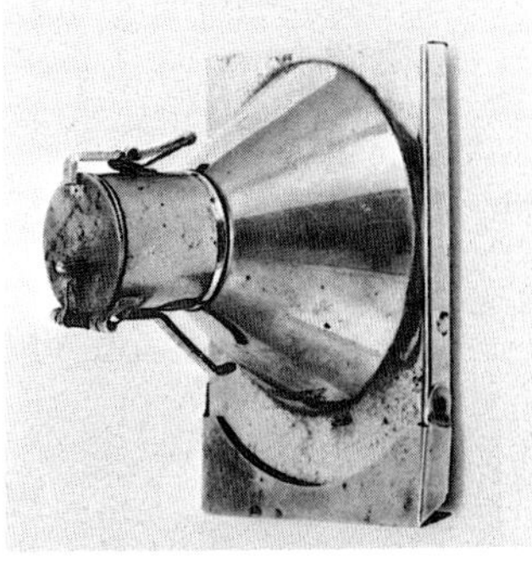

Ref	Name	Data	Average Condition Price Range £	$
ANSCO see AGFA/ANSCO				
ANTHONY (New York)				
P18	Boxform view camera 10 * 8 in.	*	a. 1500	a. 2600
P19	Tailboard 5 * 8 in.	*	a. 40	a. 70
APEM/KERSHAW/SOHO (London)				
P20	Single Lens Reflex	pcc	30-60	55-110
R21	'Curlew 11' (Critak f4.5)	**	30-35	50-60
R22	'Curlew 111'(TTH Roytal f3.8)	*	a. 75	a. 130
R23	Folding rollfilm	pcc	5-10	9-18
R24	Folding rollfilm/plate	pcc	8-15	13-25
R25	'Kershaw 630' (2 1/4 sq)	pcc	8-15	13-25
R26	'Penguin' or 'King Penguin'	pcc	5-10	9-18
R27	'Peregrine 111'	*	a. 30	a. 55
> R28	'Rajar No 6' bakelite strut	pcc	5-10	9-18
R29	'Raven' folding (8 on 120)	pcc	5-10	9-18
R30	'Soho' bakelite folding	pcc	5-10	9-18
R31	'Soho B' folding (8 on 120)	pcc	5-10	9-18
R32	'Soho Cadet' V.P.	pcc	10-20	18-35
R33	'Soho' V.P.(oxy-brass casing)	*	a. 170	a. 300
APPARATE & KAMERABAU (Germany)				
Q21	'Akarette Super P'	pcc	5-10	9-18
APPLETON (Bradford)				
P21	Field 1/2 plate	*	a. 60	a. 110
ARGUS/I.R.C (Ann Arbor USA)				
Q22	'Argus A' (black bakelite)	pcc	5-10	9-18
Q23	'Argus A3' (1940-42)	pcc	15-30	25-50
> Q24	'Argus C3' c.r.f.	pcc	10-20	18-35
Q25	'Argus C3' outfit	*	a. 40	a. 70
R34	'Argoflex' T.L.R. style	pcc	8-15	13-25
ASAHI (Tokyo)				
Q26	'Asahiflex' S.L.R.	*	a. 120	a. 220
Q27	'Heiland Pentax H1' S.L.R.	*	a. 40	a. 70
> Q28	'Pentax Spotmatic' etc.	****	75-85	130-150
ASIA AMERICAN (Tokyo)				
R35	'Orinox' binocular (110 film)	*	a. 60	a. 110

> R28. 'Rajar No 6'
... Introduced in 1929 as one of the earliest bakelite rollfilm cameras. It was made in large quantities and distributed by premium gift schemes. The number still around show its robust design. Made by APM Ltd whose camera buisness became SOHO Ltd.in 1930.

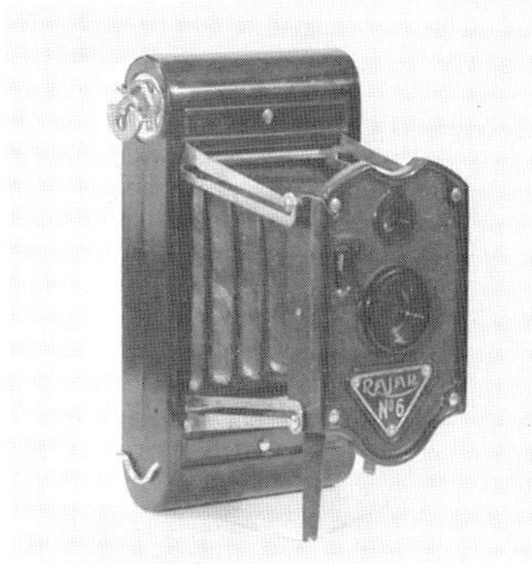

> Q24. 'Argus C3'
... The 'brick' range of 35mm cameras - so called due to their shape weight and size - started with the non coupled rangefinder 'C' in 1938. The 'C2' and 'C3' had coupled rangefinders but the latter also had internal flash synchronisation.
It was made until 1966.

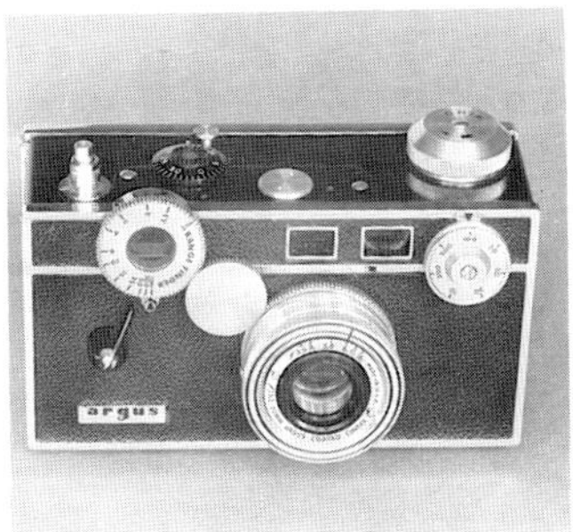

> Q28. 'Pentax Spotmatic'
... This category covers 'Spotmatics' et al of the period 1964 to 1974. The collectors price is determined by condition rather than the particular model.The name is misleading as production versions of the 'Spotmatic' had an averaging not a spot meter.

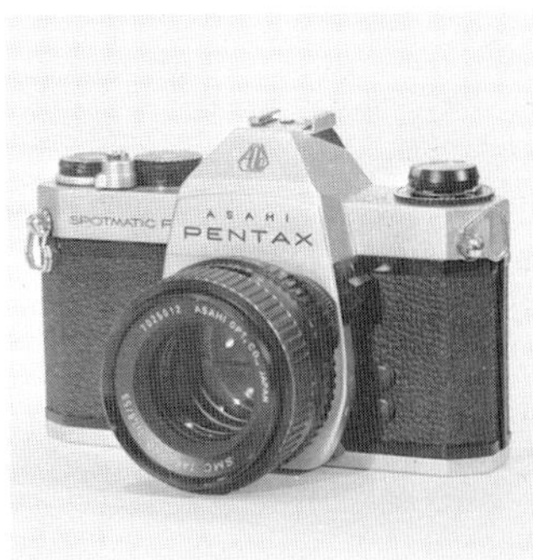

Ref	Name	Data	Average Condition Price Range £	$
ASTORIA OPTICAL (Japan)				
R36	'Astoria' c.r.f.	**	35-45	65-80
ATKINSON (Liverpool)				
P22	Tailboard 1/4 pl	*	a. 60	a. 110
ATOM OPTICAL (Japan)				
R37	'Atom Six 11' folding	**	18-20	30-35
BALDA (Dresden/Bunde)				
Q29	'Baldalette' folding	pcc	20-40	35-70
Q30	'Baldamatic' c.r.f.	pcc	15-30	25-50
Q31	'Baldessa 1b' c.r.f.	pcc	10-20	18-35
> Q32	'Baldinette' folding	pcc	8-15	13-25
Q33	'Baldini' folding	*	a. 12	a. 20
Q34	'Jubilette' folding	pcc	20-40	35-70
Q35	'Super Balda/Baldina' c.r.f.	pcc	20-40	35-70
R38	'Baldax' c.r.f.	**	18-20	30-35
R39	'Baldaxette 1' (16 on 120)	pcc	15-30	25-50
R40	'Baldi' (16 on 127)	pcc	20-40	35-70
R41	Folding c.r.f.	**	20-40	35-70
R42	'Hapo 10' folding (120 film)	pcc	10-20	18-35
R421	'Rigona' (16 on 127)	pcc	8-15	13-25
BECK R.J (London)				
P24	Boxform magazine 1/4 pl	*	a. 40	a. 70
P25	'Pecrops' field 1/2 pl	*	a. 120	a. 220
P26	Tailboard 5 * 4	*	a. 85	a. 150
R43	'Zambex' filmpack 1/4 pl	*	a. 120	a. 220
> S3	'Frena' magazine camera	****	45-50	75-85
S301	'Frena' hide covered outfit	*	a. 330	a. 550
BEIER (Freital by Dresden)				
Q36	'Beira' c.r.f	*	a. 65	a. 110
Q37	'Beirette' folding	*	a. 30	a. 55
> Q38	'Beirette' (rigid type)	pcc	5-10	9-18
Q39	'Beirette Junior'	pcc	5-10	9-18
R44	Folding c.r.f	pcc	20-40	35-70
BELCA (Dresden)				
R45	'Belfoca' folding	pcc	8-15	13-25
BELL & HOWELL (Chicago)				
Q40	'Foton' (motor driven)	***	140-170	240-300

> Q32. 'Baldinette'
... A folding 35 mm. camera c.1950 similar in design to the Kodak 'Retina' as were the 'Baldina' of the 1930's and the later 'Baldini'. All these cameras were fitted with various lens/shutter combinations. This category excludes the Super c.r.f. models.

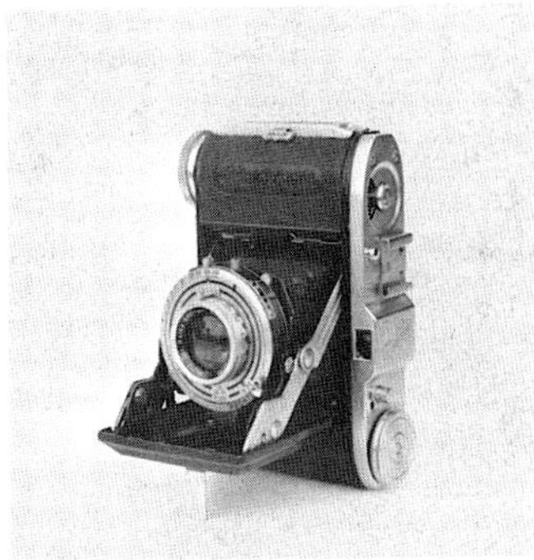

> S3. 'Frena'
... The 'Frena' was a hybrid design of falling plate and cut-film. Special notched sheet film was carried in a rotatable holder. After exposure the film fell to the bottom by gravity when the control was manipulated. The 'Frena' range was made c.1892 for several years.

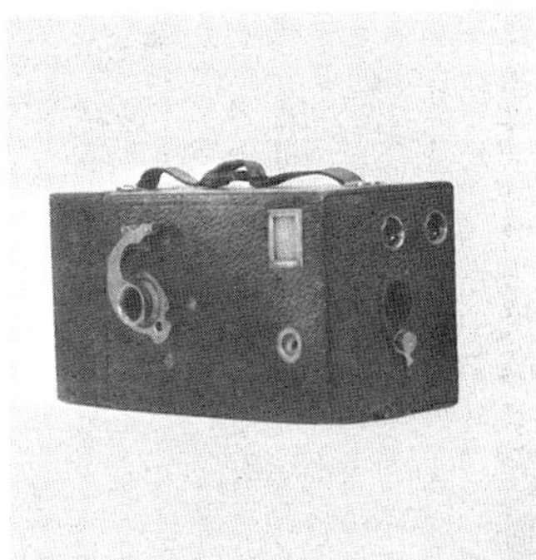

> Q38. 'Beirette' (rigid)
... This category covers the 1960's range of low cost 35 mm. cameras manufactured in East Germany. It should not be confused with the much more collectable folding camera of the same name c. 1938. Included are the Beirette K which took Rapid cassettes and the VSN.

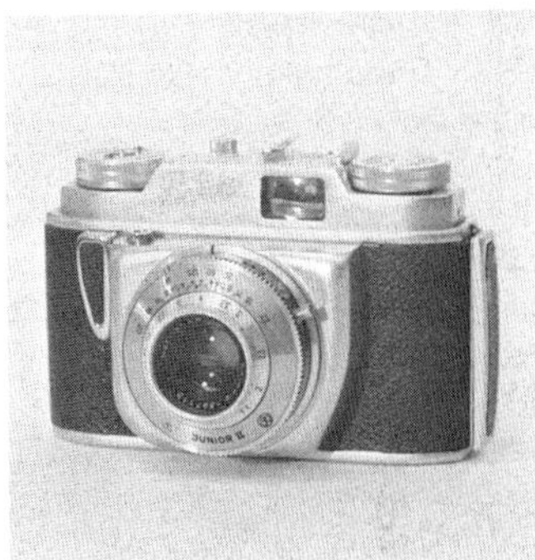

Ref	Name	Data	Average Condition Price Range £	$
Q41	'Stereo Colorist'	*	a. 80	a. 140
Q42	'Stereo Colorist 2'(rangef'dr)	*	a. 130	a. 220
R46	'Autoload' (126 film)	pcc	5-10	9-18
BELLIENI (Nancy)				
P27	Stereo jumelle 6 * 13 cm	**	75-90	130-160
P28	Strut folding 6.5 * 9 cm.	*	a. 45	a. 80
BENCINI (Italy)				
> R47	'Comet' rigid body (127 film)	pcc	8-15	13-25
R48	'Comet 111' c.r.f.	**	18-20	30-35
R49	'Koroll' (12 on 120)	pcc	5-10	9-18
BENETFINK (London)				
P29	Falling plate T.L.R. 1/4 pl	*	a. 140	a. 240
P30	'Lightning' falling plate	*	a. 20	a. 35
BENTZIN/PRIMAR (Goerlitz)				
P31	Stereo strut	*	a. 150	a. 260
> R50	'Primarflex' S.L.R.	***	90-110	160-200
R51	'Primarette' V.P. twin lens	*	a. 380	a. 650
BERNING (Dusseldorf)				
Q43	'Robot 1' motor wind	***	100-120	170-200
Q44	'Robot' 11.11A. & Junior	****	60-75	110-130
Q45	'Robot Luftwaffen'	****	85-100	140-170
Q46	'Robot Recorder'	***	80-100	140-170
Q47	'Robot Royal'	**	170-200	280-340
> Q48	'Robot Star'	**	55-65	95-120
Q49	'Robot Vollutomat'	***	120-150	220-260
BILLCLIFF (Manchester)				
P32	Field 1/2 plate	**	55-65	95-120
P33	Tailboard 1/4 plate	**	60-75	110-130
P34	Wet plate studio & stand	*	a. 340	a. 600
BILORA (Germany)				
Q50	'Radix' (Biloxar f5.6)	pcc	10-20	18-35
R52	'Boy' brown bakelite box	pcc	8-15	13-25
BILUX/IDAM (France)				
R53	'Clic' cast metal 3 * 3 cm	*	a. 30	a. 55
BLAIR (Boston Mass.)				
P35	'Combination' 5 * 4 in.	*	a. 120	a. 220

> R47. 'Comet 1 11 and S' ... A range of cast aluminium bodied miniature cameras for 12 (4*4 cm) or 16 (3*4 cm) on 127 film sold during the 1950's and 1960's by Boot's. Model 1 was fixed focus;Model 11 helical focus Model S was flash sync. Not to be confused with R48 which is vertically styled.

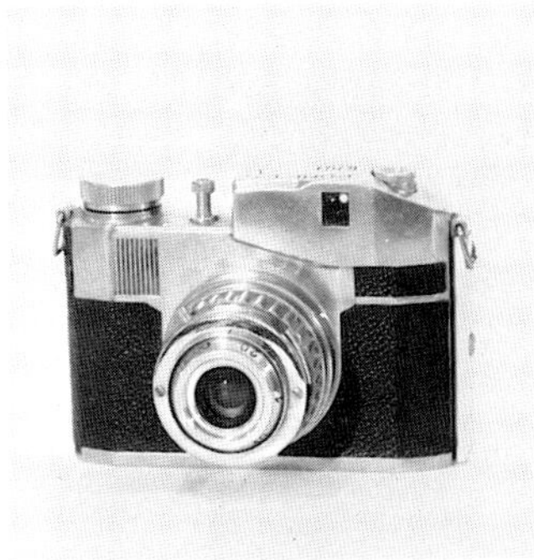

> R50. 'Primarflex' S.L.R. ... For 6 * 6 cm (12 on 120 film or plates). c. 1935. Similar in design to the Hasselblad but pre-dating it by 13 years. Continued after WW 2 as the Primar Reflex. The 'Primarflex 11' (or in the U.S. 'Astraflex 11') appeared c.1951 with interchangeable finder hood.

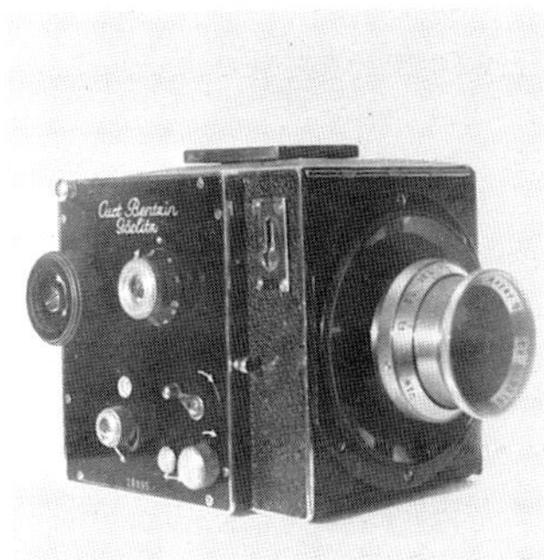

> Q48. 'Robot Star/Star 11' ... This robust and long lived series of motorised 35 mm. cameras was introduced in 1934 and a version is still in production.
The 'Robot Star' c.1952 to 1959 with f1.9 Xenon was followed c.1960 by the 'Robot Star 11'.

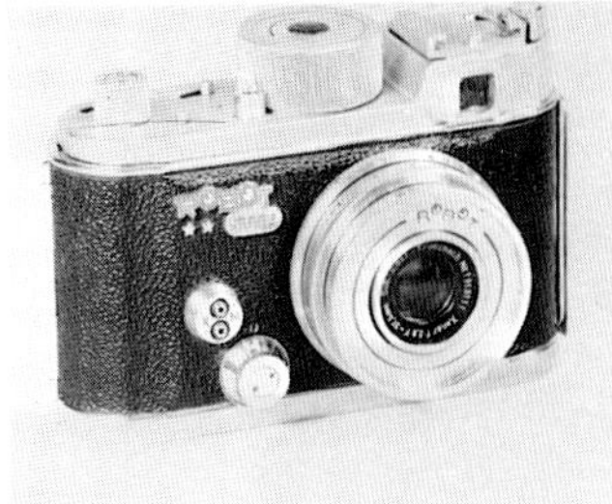

BLAIR (Boston Mass.)(cont'd)

Ref	Name	Data	Average Condition Price Range £	$
P351	'Century' folding 1/4 pl	**	45-55	80-100
R55	'Stereo Hawkeye' 3 1/2 in sq.	***	130-160	220-260
R56	'Stereo Weno' 3 1/2 in. sq.	***	100-120	170-200
BLOCH (Paris)				
P36	'Le Physiographe' stereo	***	460-550	800-1000
BOLCO (London)				
R57	'Bolco VP Twin' (16 on 127)	pcc	5-10	9-18
BOLSEY (New York)				
Q51	'Bolsey B2'	pcc	15-30	25-50
BOLTA/PHOTOAVIT-WERK (Nuernberg)				
Q52	'Photoavit' compact 35mm.	***	25-30	45-55
> R58	'Boltavit' 25 * 25 mm	*	a. 70	a. 120
R59	'Photina' T.L.R.	pcc	8-15	13-25
BOLTON & BARNITT (London)				
P37	Sliding box wet plate	*	a. 700	a. 1200
BOOTS (Nottingham)				
P38	Field 1/4 plate	*	a. 200	a. 360
BOUMSELL (Paris)				
R60	'Photo-Magic' bakelite box	pcc	8-15	13-25
BOURDIN (Paris)				
> P39	'Dubroni' wet plate camera	***	700-850	1200-1500
P40	'Dubroni' outfits	***	3500-4300	6200-7600
BOYER (France)				
R61	Bakelite camera	pcc	Under 5	Under 9
B.P. Co (Birmingham)				
P41	'Criterion' boxform 1/16 pl.	*	a. 100	a. 180
BRADAC (Czechoslovakia)				
R62	'Kamarad M11' T.L.R.	*	a. 18	a. 30
BRAUN (Nuernberg)				
Q53	'Paxette' simple compact	pcc	5-10	9-18
Q54	'Paxina 35'	pcc	8-15	13-25
> Q55	'Super Paxette' c.r.f.	**	18-20	30-35
R63	'Gloria' (uncoupled r.f.)	pcc	10-20	18-35
R64	'Imperial' box	pcc	Under 5	Under 9
R65	'Paxette 28BX' (126 film)	pcc	5-10	9-18
R66	'Paxina'	pcc	5-10	9-18

> R58. 'Boltavit'
... Miniature cast metal body camera finished black or chrome with black leather front panel. It took 25 * 25 mm exposures on special rollfilm. Lenses either f7.7 Doppel-Objectiv or f4.5 Corygon. Introduced c.1936 it was followed c.1937 by the similar rollfilm 'Photavit'.

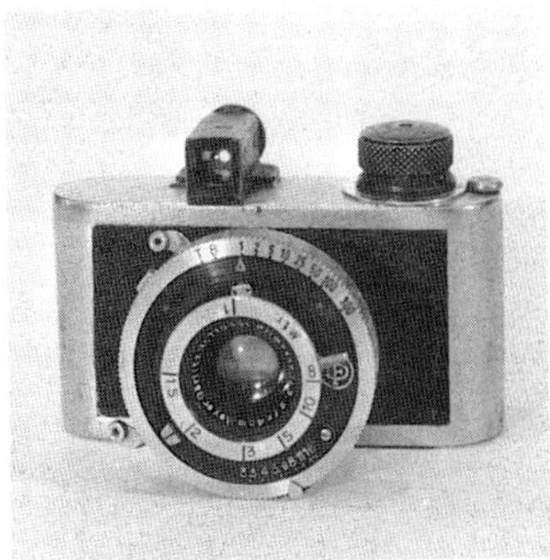

> P39. 'Dubroni'
... The first popular camera to internally process wet collodion plates. The coated plate was placed inside; the silver nitrate solution introduced via a pipette flowed over the glass plate. Post exposure processing was carried out in a similar fashion. c.1860's

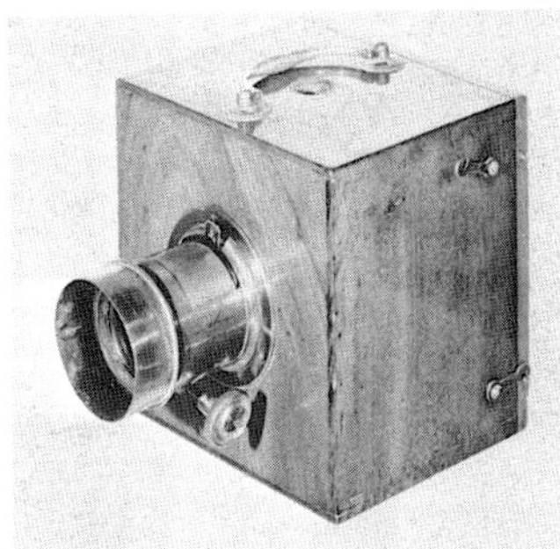

> Q55. 'Super Paxette'
... A range of coupled rangefinder cameras of the 1950's and 1960's designated 1 1B 11 11B and 11BL. The range of interchangeable lenses in Pronto series shutters included f2.8 45 mm. Staeble-Kata; f2.8 50 mm Color-Ultralit; Tessar f2.8 50 mm; and Xenar f2.8 50 mm.

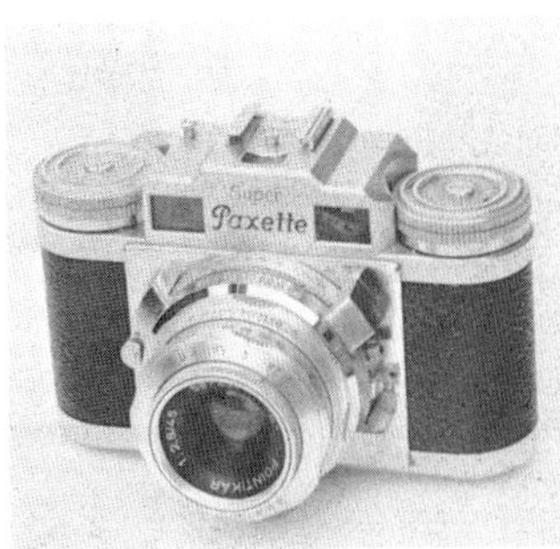

Ref	Name	Data	Average Condition Price Range £	$
BROWN J.E (England)				
P42	'Patent Combination Field'	*	a. 100	a. 180
BROWN N (London)				
> S4	'Nebro' extinction meter	pcc	5-10	9-18
BRUNS (Munich)				
P43	'Patent Magazine'	*	a. 2200	a. 3900
BULLARD (Springfield MA)				
P44	Hand and Stand	**	45-55	80-100
BUSCH (Germany)				
P45	'Beecam' folding 1/4 plate	*	a. 75	a. 130
P46	'Beecam' stereo 2.5 * 6.5 in	*	a. 90	a. 160
R67	Folding (early style)	**	50-60	85-100
BUTCHER (London)				
P47	'Cameo' folding plate	pcc	15-30	25-50
P48	'Klimax' folding plate	**	20-25	35-45
P49	'Midg' falling plate	**	30-35	50-60
P50	'Midg' folding falling plate	**	60-75	110-130
P51	'National' 1/2 pl field	***	70-85	120-150
P52	'Pilot No 2' falling plate	*	a. 35	a. 60
P53	'Popular Pressman' reflex	**	60-75	110-130
P54	'Primus' detective 5 * 4 in.	*	a. 30	a. 55
P55	'Primus' folding	**	20-25	35-45
P56	'Stereo Cameo' 7 * 3 1/2 in	*	a. 150	a. 260
> P57	'Stereolette' 45 * 107 mm.	**	85-100	140-170
R68	'Box Carbine No 2'	pcc	5-10	9-18
R69	'Maxim' box	pcc	10-20	18-35
R70	'Stereo Rollfilm Carbine'	*	a. 150	a. 260
R71	'Watch Pocket Carbine'	pcc	10-20	18-35
S5	'Dandycam' ferrotype camera	*	a. 240	a. 420
S6	'Welbourne-Piper Stop Clock'	*	a. 120	a. 220
CAILLON (Paris)				
P58	'Bioscope' jumelle stereo	*	a. 85	a. 150
P59	'Megascope' jumelle stereo	*	a. 60	a. 110
P60	'Scopea' jumelle stereo	*	a. 60	a. 110
CAMERA CORPN. (Chicago)				
Q56	'Perfex Fifty-five' c.r.f.	**	25-30	45-55

> S4. 'Nebro' exposure meter ... A British made extinction type exposure meter sold by NEVILLE BROWN. It was well designed and easy to use and was deservedly popular for many years. c.1920's/1930's.

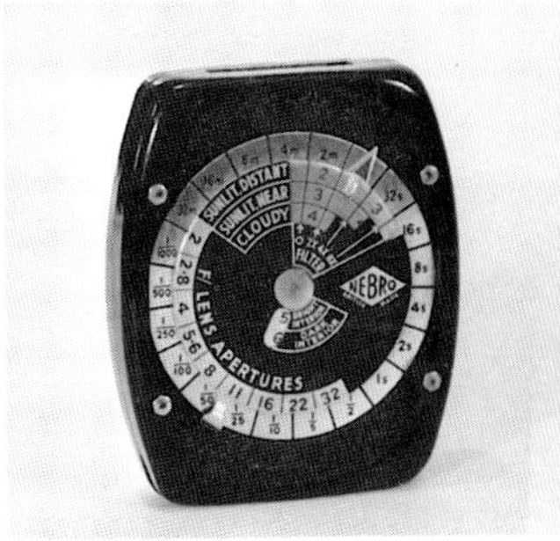

> P57. 'Stereolette' ... A folding 45 * 107 mm stereo camera made by ICA for BUTCHERS. It resembles two V.P. 'Klimax' folding plate cameras on a common bedplate with rack and pinion focussing and a small rise to the lens panel. Made with several lens/shutter combinations. c.1910.

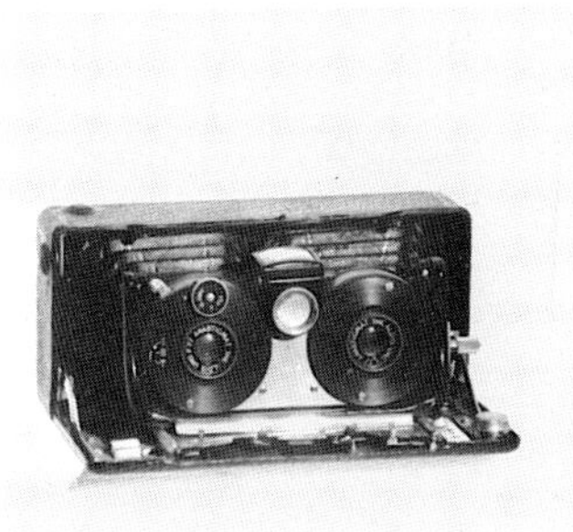

---

* THE PHOTOGRAPHIC COLLECTORS CLUB of G.B. *

Founded 1977 the PCC GB now has a worldwide membership of over 700. Regular meetings are held at venues round the country. A Journal is issued and a postal auction held quarterly and a 'Photographica' fair annually. Details available from :- The Membership Secretary. PCC GB
P.O. Box 127a Surbiton Surrey. KT6 7EE. England

Ref	Name	Data	Average Condition Price Range £	$
CAMOJECT (London)				
> S7	'Camoject' sub-miniature	**	40-50	70-85
CANON (Tokyo)				
Q57	'Canonette' rangefinder	pcc	10-20	18-35
Q58	'Canonflex' S.L.R.	*	a. 65	a. 110
Q59	'Canon EE.EX' S.L.R.	*	a. 35	a. 60
Q60	'Canon' (Leica copies)	***	100-120	170-200
Q61	'Canon FD' S.L.R	**	60-75	100-120
Q62	'Canon FT' S.L.R.	**	65-80	110-130
Q63	'Canon FX' body only	pcc	15-30	25-50
> Q64	'Canon FX' S.L.R.	*	a. 40	a. 70
Q65	'Canon P' c.r.f.	*	a. 75	a. 130
Q66	'Canon S' c.r.f.	*	a. 900	a. 1600
Q67	'Canon S2' c.r.f.	**	200-240	340-420
Q68	'Canon VT' c.r.f.	***	140-170	240-300
Q69	'Canon VTDM' c.r.f.	*	a. 240	a. 420
Q70	'Canon V1-T' c.r.f.	*	a. 180	a. 320
Q71	'Canon 11 to 11F'(Leica copy)	***	120-150	220-260
Q72	'Canon 111/111a'(Leica copy)	***	60-75	110-130
Q73	'Canon 1V F' c.r.f	**	200-240	340-420
Q74	'Canon 1V S' c.r.f	pcc	100-200	180-360
Q75	'Canon 1V SB' c.r.f	**	85-100	140-170
Q76	'Canon 7' c.r.f	**	170-200	280-340
Q77	'Canon 7' body only	pcc	50-100	90-180
Q78	'Demi' half frame	pcc	15-30	25-50
Q79	'Dial' half frame	***	25-30	45-55
Q80	'Pellix' S.L.R.	***	70-85	120-150
Q81	'Populaire' (with canonmeter)	*	a. 180	a. 320
R72	'Canonmatic C30' (126)	pcc	8-15	13-25
CARPENTIER see London Stereo				
CENTURY (New York)				
P61	Hand and Stand 5 * 4 in.	**	90-110	160-200
CERTO (Dresden)				
P62	'Certotrop' folding	**	25-30	45-55
Q82	'Dollina 1'	**	15-18	25-30
> Q83	'Dollina' (c.r.f.)	**	25-30	45-55

> S7. 'Camoject' ... Made c.1955 of moulded black plastic. It was supplied pre-loaded with film; after use the back of the camera was returned to the makers for reloading. Winding was by a coin in a slot guesstimating the turns as there was no way of counting exposures.

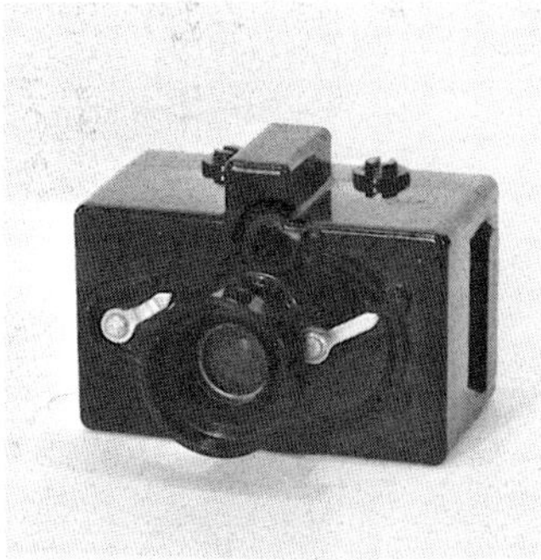

> Q64. 'Canon FX' S.L.R. ... c.1964 to 1966. The 'FX'is a comparatively rare derivative of the '7s' with similar focal plane shutter and semi - coupled cds metering systems. But the 'FX' used the FL series breech lock lenses and a reflex system with mirror lock up.

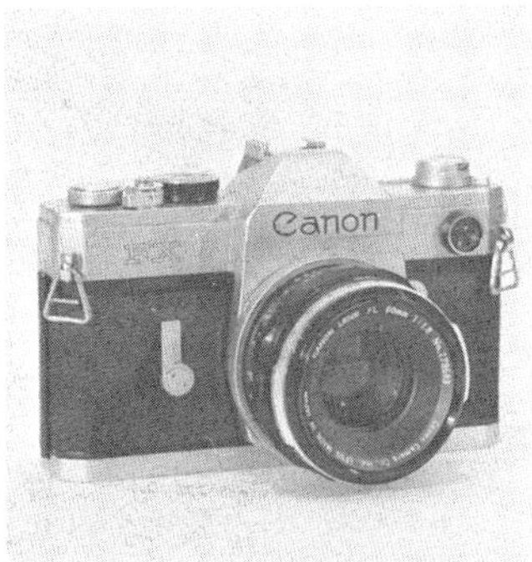

> Q83. 'Dollina 11 & 111' ... The coupled rangefinder versions of the 'Dollina' were introduced in 1936. The rangefinder housing of the 11 and 111 differ the latter being the larger.
The usual lenses were Xenon f2; Tessar f2.8; Xenar f2.9 or Radionar f2.9. in Compur or Compur Rapid shutter.

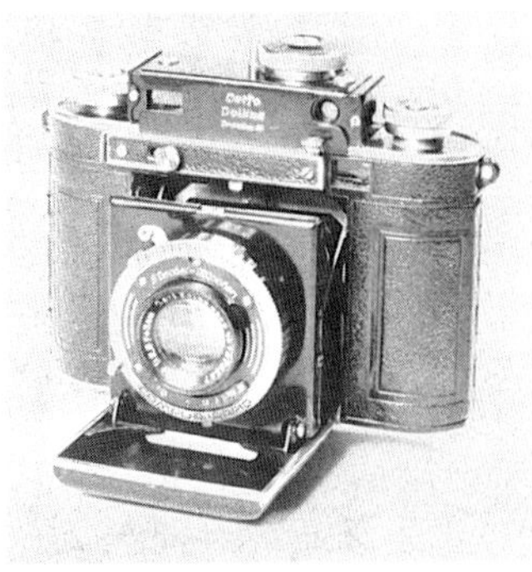

CERTO (Dresden)(cont'd)

Ref	Name	Data	Average Condition Price Range £	$
R73	'Certo-phot' (12 on 120)	pcc	5-10	9-18
R74	'Dolly' (127 film)	**	65-80	110-130
R75	'Dolly Super Sports' c.r.f	pcc	20-40	35-70
CHADWICK W.I (Machester)				
P63	Tailboard 1/2 plate	**	80-100	140-170
P64	Tailboard stereo 1/2 pl	**	280-340	480-600
CHAPMAN J.T (Manchester)				
P65	'Britsh' detective	**	55-65	95-120
P66	'British' falling plate	**	50-60	85-100
P67	'British' field 1/4 plate	**	90-110	160-200
P68	'British' field 1/2 plate	***	130-160	220-260
P69	Hand & Stand 1/4 & 1/2 pl	**	65-80	110-130
P70	Magazine (Millers Patent)	*	a. 40	a. 70
P71	Stereo field 1/2 plate	*	a. 220	a. 380
CHESNAU (Marseille)				
P72	Boxform detective 1/4 pl	*	a. 25	a. 45
CHEVALIER (Paris)				
P73	Daguerrotype (folding) outfit	*	a. 11000	a. 19500
CHICAGO FERROTYPE (Chicago)				
S8	'Wonder Photo Cannon'	**	200-240	340-420
CHINESE (Shanghai)				
Q84	'Red Flag 20' (Leica M4 copy)	*	a. 3000	a. 5300
CHIYODA/MINOLTA (Tokyo)				
Q85	'Minolta'S.L.R. (most types)	***	55-65	95-120
Q86	'SRM' S.L.R.	*	a. 100	a. 180
Q87	'XE-5' S.L.R.	*	a. 240	a. 420
R76	Compact '110 Zoom'	pcc	30-60	55-110
CHRISTIN PHOTO (New York)				
S9	'Insta' (Polaroid competitor)	*	a. 60	a. 110
CIE FRANCAIS de PHOTO.(Paris)				
> P74	'Photosphere'	**	700-850	1200-1500
CITY SALE & EXCHANGE see SALEX				
COLUMBIA CAMERA (London)				
> P75	'Pecto' Hand & Stand	**	45-55	80-100
CONCAVA (Lugano)				
> Q88	'Tessina' miniature T.L.R.	****	180-200	300-340

> P74. 'Photosphere'
... A peculiarly shaped all metal French camera. The flat back took either double dark slides or a magazine changer and was fitted to a bell shaped housing carrying the lens and shutter. It was made in several sizes and in a stereo version. c. 1888.

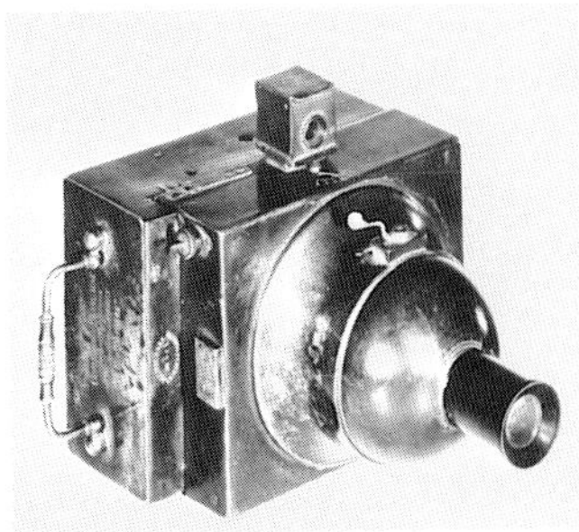

> P75. 'Pecto'
... Although supplied by The COLUMBIA CAMERA Co. of London it is obviously of American origin. It was a well made hand & stand camera with spring-back red leather bellows and a polished wood interior. It was covered in heavy grade leather. 5 * 4 or 7 * 5 in.

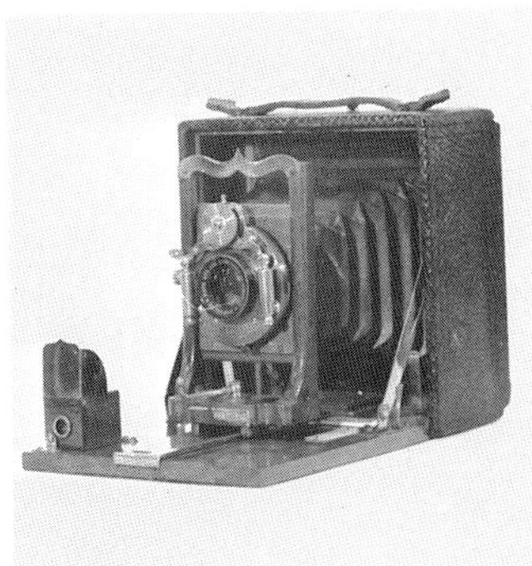

> Q88. 'Tessina'
... Unusual miniature T.L.R. taking 14 * 21 mm images on 35 mm film in special cartridges. Semi-automatic operation with spring motor wind taking 5 to 8 frames per winding. Available from 1960 to the present finished in chrome; black; red and gold (in order of value).

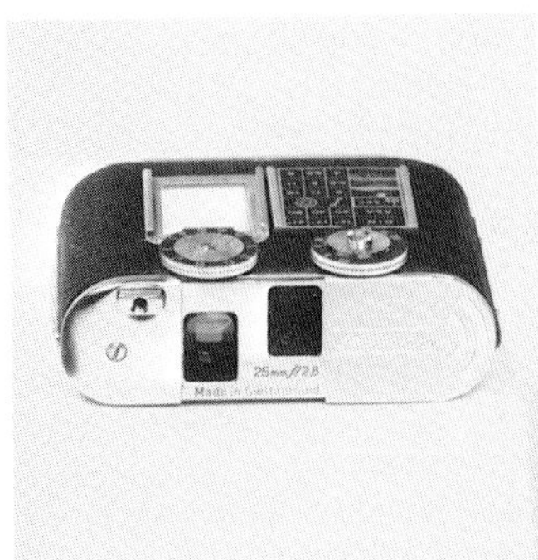

CONLEY (Rochester N.Y.)

Ref	Name	Data	Average Condition Price Range £	$
CONLEY (Rochester N.Y.)				
P76	Hand and Stand 5 * 4 in	**	50-60	85-100
CONTESSA-NETTEL (Stuttgart)				
P77	'Clarissa' strut trop. V.P.	*	a. 700	a. 1200
P78	Folding trop. 4.5 * 6 cm.	**	650-800	1100-1300
P79	'Sonnar' folding 9 * 12 cm.	**	20-25	35-45
R77	Folding rollfilm	pcc	10-20	18-35
CONTESSA-NETTEL/Z.I (Stuttgart)				
P80	'Adoro' tropical	***	180-220	320-400
P81	'Citoskop Stereo'	*	a. 95	a. 170
> P82	Deckrullo 9 * 12 cm strut	*	a. 75	a. 130
P83	Deckrullo tropical	**	360-440	650-800
P84	'Donata' folding plate	**	25-30	45-55
P85	'Duchessa' stereo	**	130-160	220-260
P86	'Ergo' 4.5 * 6 cm	*	a. 320	a. 550
P87	'Miroflex' folding S.L.R.	**	60-75	110-130
P88	'Sonnet' tropical 6.5 * 9 cm.	**	240-300	420-500
P89	'Sonnet' tropical 4.5 * 6 cm	**	460-550	800-1000
P90	'Tessco' folding 6 * 9 cm.	*	a. 35	a. 60
> R78	'Cocarette' 6 * 9 cm.	**	25-30	45-55
R79	'Cocarette Luxus' (brown)	**	85-100	140-170
R80	'Picolette' folding V.P.	**	35-45	65-80
R81	'Picolette Luxus' V.P.	*	a. 260	a. 460
CORFIELD (Wolverhampton)				
Q89	'Periflex' S.L.R.	****	50-60	85-100
Q90	'Periflex' outfit	*	a. 110	a. 190
R82	'Corfield 66' S.L.R.	****	80-100	140-170
CORNU (Paris)				
P91	'Ontoscope' stereo	**	200-240	340-420
R83	'Ontoflex' T.L.R.	*	a. 150	a. 260
CORONET (Birmingham)				
> P92	'Coronet' box outfit	*	a. 12	a. 20
P93	Field 1/2 plate	**	65-80	110-130
R84	'Cameo'bakelite 13 * 18 cm.	**	25-30	45-55
R85	'Coronet 3D'(4 pairs on 127)	***	25-30	45-55
R86	'Cub' 28 * 40 mm (828 film)	pcc	5-10	9-18

> P82. 'Deckrullo'
... A 1920's classic German folding press camera with the facility of scale focussing before pulling out the lens board. It had external scissor struts and later models also had internal trellis struts.
On early versions the f.p.s. was speeded to 1/2800 sec.

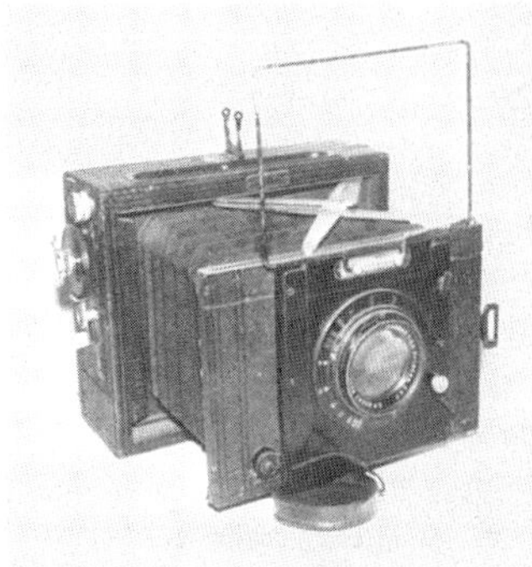

> R78. 'Cocarette'
... Originally made by CONTESSA NETTEL it continued as a cheaper end of the market folder by ZEISS IKON until 1931. Several models in the 6 * 9 cm size with a range of lenses and shutters and various finishes.
Not to be confused with the brown Luxus at R79.

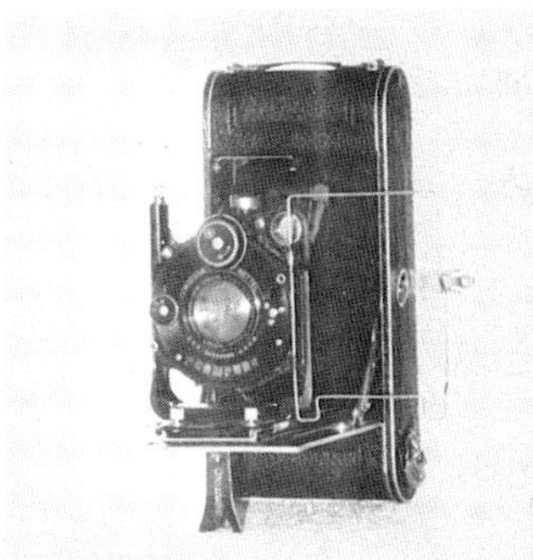

> P92. 'Coronet' outfit
... Purchased as a complete outfit comprising the cardboard camera a small plate with card holder and a printing frame made of paper together with all the chemicals required to make a poor quality print (which quickly faded from inadequate fixing). c.1930's

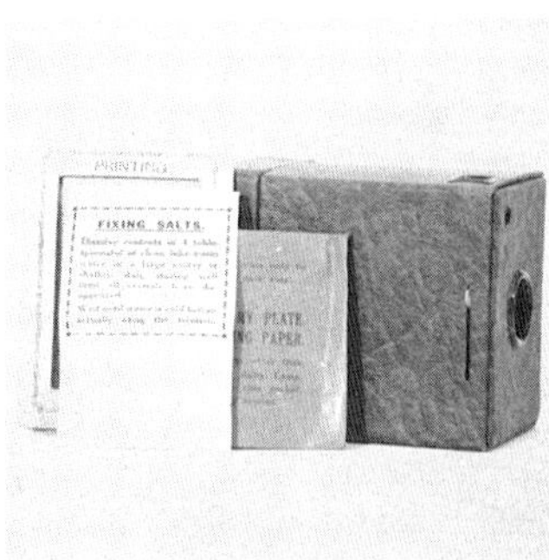

CORONET (Birmingham)(cont'd)

Ref	Name	Data	Average Condition Price Range £	$
R87	Folding rollfilm	pcc	5-10	9-18
R88	'Outspan' box (8 on 120)	pcc	Under 5	Under 9
R89	'Popular 12' box	pcc	Under 5	Under 9
R90	'Rapide' folding (12 on 120)	pcc	Under 5	Under 9
R91	'Rapier' folding	pcc	5-10	9-18
R92	'Six Three'	pcc	Under 5	Under 9
R93	'Viscount' folding	pcc	5-10	9-18
> R94	'Vogue' brown bakelite	**	18-20	30-35
R95	Folding '4-4' (12 on 127)	pcc	Under 5	Under 9
> S10	'Midget' (most variants)	*****	40-50	75-90
S11	'Midget' (rarer variants)	***	80-100	140-170
CORONET (France)				
R96	'Fildia'	pcc	Under 5	Under 9
COX F.J (England)				
P94	Wet plate sliding box outfit	*	a. 1800	a. 3200
DACORA (Munich)				
Q91	Folding c.r.f.	pcc	8-15	13-25
R97	'Daci' box	pcc	Under 5	Under 9
DALLMEYER (London)				
P95	'Correspondent' H & S 5 * 4	*	a. 110	a. 190
P96	Field 1/2 plate or 5 * 4 in.	**	110-130	190-240
P97	'Naturalist' reflex 1/4 pl.	*	a. 380	a. 650
P98	Single Lens Reflex 1/4 pl.	*	a. 20	a. 35
> P99	'Speed' 4.5 * 6 cm.	***	130-160	220-260
P100	'Speed' 1/4 pl or 6.5 * 9 cm.	***	70-85	120-150
P101	Tailboard 1/2 or 1/1 plate	**	140-170	240-300
P102	Wet plate sliding-box stereo	***	1400-1700	2400-2900
R98	'Dual' folding (16 on 120)	*	a. 95	a. 170
R99	'Snapshot' filmpack 6 * 9cm	**	25-30	45-55
DANCER (Manchester)				
P103	Tailboard 1/2 plate	*	a. 85	a. 150
DAWES (London)				
P104	'Nelrod Liteflash' 5 * 4 in.	*	a. 70	a. 120
DEBRIE (Paris)				
Q92	'Sept' (f3.5 Stylor)	pcc	100-200	180-360

> R94 'Vogue'
... Miniature brown bakelite self-erecting bellows camera c.1936. It used special Vogue 35 film to take 12 exposures 2 * 1 1/2 in. This film was similar to Kodak's 828 and was used by CORONET in some inexpensive small cameras e.g. the 'Coronet Cub' c.1937.

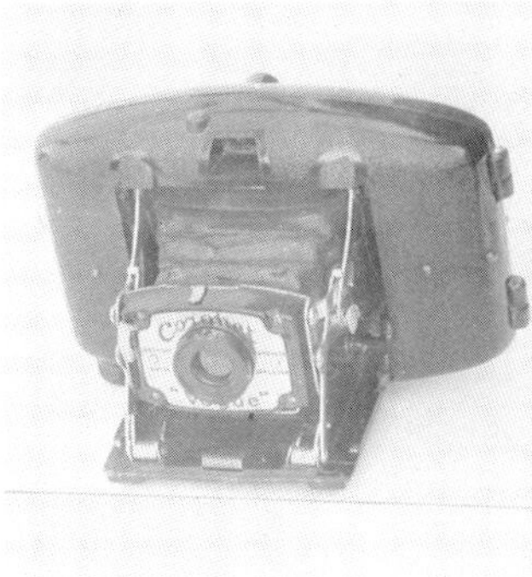

> S10. 'Midget'
... Made in Birmingham the CORONET 'Midget took 6 exposures on special 16mm roll film. Its only virtue was the bakelite moulding in 5 colours which now make it collectable. Scarcest are the blue and brown variants whilst black ones are the most common. c. 1935.

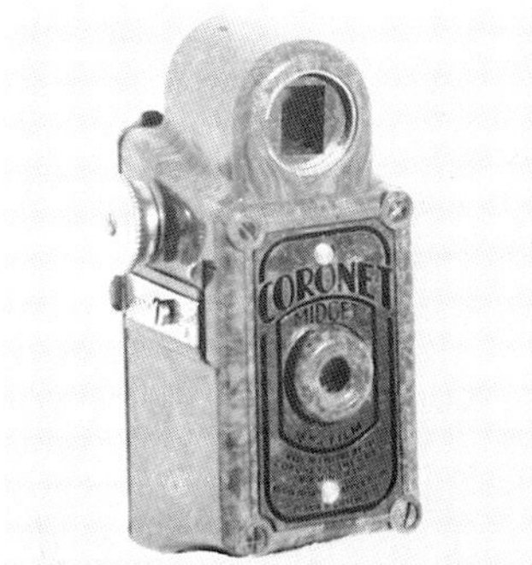

> P99. 'Speed'
... Made by NEWMAN and and GUARDIA for DALLMEYER's new high speed lens the f2.9 Pentac which was the purpose and hence the name of the camera. The f.p.s was that of the N & G Folding Reflex and the rest of 'Sibyl' origin. The larger sizes are at ref. Q100. c.1926.

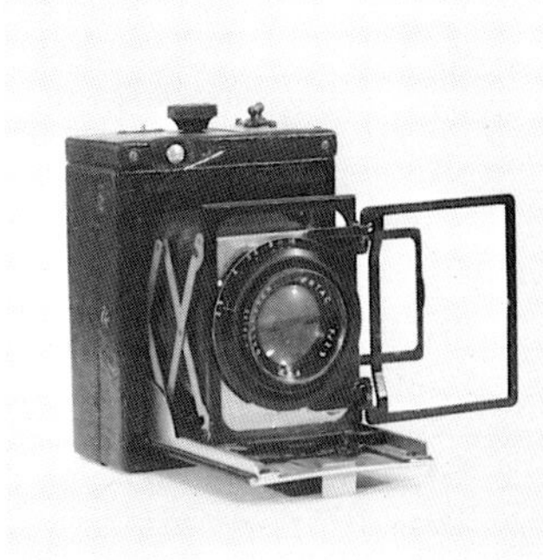

DECOUDIN (Paris)

Ref	Name	Data	Average Condition Price Range £	$
S12	Photometer exposure meter	*	a. 120	a. 220
DE JUR-AMSCO (New York)				
Q93	'D3' c.r.f.	pcc	20-40	35-70
DEROGY (Paris)				
P105	View camera 1/2 plate	**	40-50	70-85
DONKER (Amsterdam)				
P106	Tailboard 1/1 plate	**	50-60	85-100
DUCATI (Milan)				
Q94	'Ducati' (rangefinder)	*	a. 60	a. 110
Q95	'Simplex' 15 exp. c.r.f.	*	a. 60	a. 110
DURST (Italy)				
> Q96	'Duca'(cine camera style)	**	16-20	30-35
R100	'Gil' box (12 on 120)	pcc	Under 5	Under 9
DZERZHINSKY/FED (Kharkov)				
Q97	'Fed'(Fed lens) Leica copy	**	35-45	65-80
Q98	'Fed'(Leitz lens) Leica copy	*	a. 80	a. 140
EASTMAN see KODAK				
EBNER (Stuttgart)				
R101	'Slimline' bakelite folding	**	55-65	95-120
EHO-ALTISSA (Dresden)				
Q99	'Altix-N'	pcc	5-10	9-18
R102	'Altiflex' T.L.R.	pcc	8-15	13-25
R103	'Altiscop' stereo (120 film)	*	a. 60	a. 110
ELMO (Japan)				
R104	'Elmoflex' T.L.R.	**	25-30	45-55
ERAC see ROBINSON E.				
ENGLISH (Maker unknown)				
R105	'Pic' (circular bakelite)	**	40-50	70-85
ENSIGN see HOUGHTON				
ERNEMANN (Dresden)				
P108	Boxform 4.5 * 6 cm.	*	a. 75	a. 130
P109	Folding 9 * 12 cm	pcc	5-10	9-18
P110	Folding reflex	*	a. 90	a. 160
P111	Hand & Stand tropical	*	a. 200	a. 360
P112	'Heag 1X' stereo strut	*	a. 100	a. 180
> P113	'Heag XV' folding 4.5 * 6 cm.	**	120-150	220-260

> Q96. 'Duca'
... This 35mm still camera is easily mistaken at first glance for a small cine camera. It gave 12 exposures 24 * 36 mm on standard stock in Agfa-Rapid cassettes. Ducar f11 50mm lens with zone focussing in simple T and I shutter. Made c.1946 to 1950.

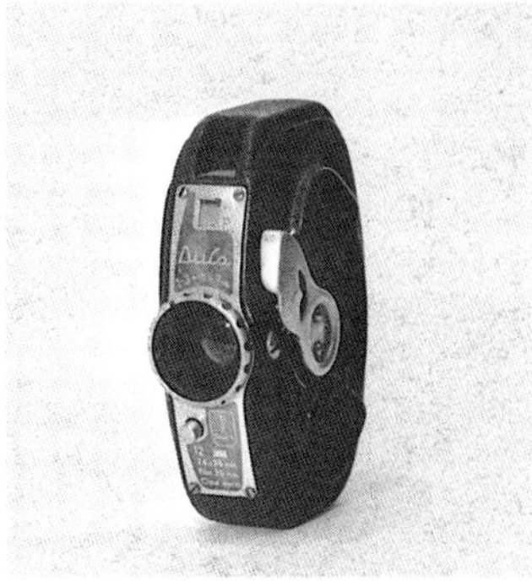

> P113. 'Heag XV' V.P.
... 'Heag XV' is the general type name for the folding V.P ERNEMANN. Made in several versions with one or two viewfinders on the baseboard and several lens/shutter combinations. All were well made and being V.P. size very pocketable. c.1905.

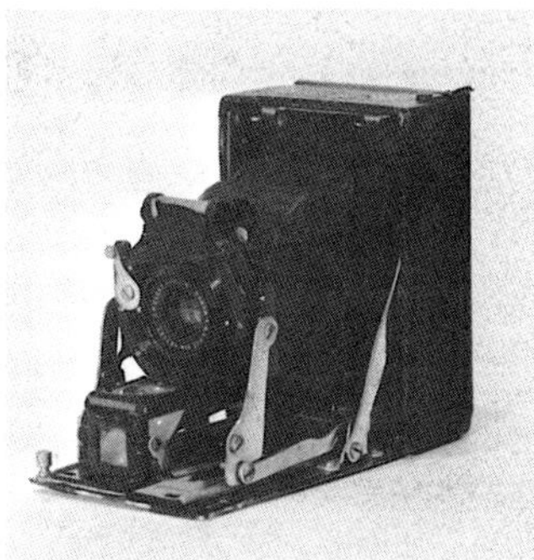

ERNEMANN (Dresden)(cont'd)

Ref	Name	Data	Average Condition Price Range £	$
P114	'Lilliput' strut 6 * 4.5 cm.	***	55-65	95-120
P115	Strut 6.5 * 9 cm.	*	a. 35	a. 60
P116	Strut tropical 9 * 12 cm	**	180-220	320-400
R106	'Bob XV' stereo 45 * 107 mm	**	150-180	260-320
R107	'Rolf 1' folding V.P.	*	a. 35	a. 60
ERNEMANN/ZEISS IKON (Dresden)				
> P117	'Ermanox' 4.5 * 6 cm	***	550-650	950-1200
P118	'Ermanox' 6.5 * 9 cm	**	700-850	1200-1500
> P119	'Ermanox' S.L.R. 4.5 * 6 cm.	**	340-420	600-750
P120	'Ernoflex' S.L.R. (not V.P.)	***	130-160	220-260
P121	'Heag 1' folding plate	pcc	15-30	25-50
P122	'Heag VI'double shutter outfit	*	a. 75	a. 130
P123	'Klapp' strut press 6.5 * 9 cm	**	65-80	110-130
R108	'Bob' folding 6 * 9 cm	pcc	10-20	18-35
R109	'Bobette 1' strut 22 * 33 mm	**	65-80	110-130
R110	'Film K' box	pcc	10-20	18-35
EVES (Leamington Spa)				
P124	One-shot beam-splitter camera	*	a. 550	a. 950
EXPO/HOUGHTON (New York/London)				
> S13	'Expo'/'Ticka' watch camera	*****	100-110	170-190
S14	'Ticka' silver monogrammed	*	a. 750	a. 1300
FALLOWFIELD (London)				
P125	'Facile' magazine 1/4 pl.	***	280-340	480-600
P126	Folding wet plate 5 * 4 in.	*	a. 300	a. 550
P127	'Peritus No 1' field	**	80-100	140-170
P128	Tailboard 8 * 12 in	*	a. 130	a. 220
P129	Tailboard Meagher type	**	100-120	170-200
P130	'Victoria' 1/2 pl field	*	a. 100	a. 180
FED see DZERZHINSKY				
FEINWERK TECHNIC (W.Germany)				
S15	'Mec-16' sub-miniature	**	35-45	65-80
FERRANIA (Milan)				
Q100	'Condor 1' c.r.f.	pcc	20-40	35-70
R111	'Elioflex' T.L.R.	pcc	5-10	9-18
R112	'Rondine' box (8 on 127)	pcc	Under 5	Under 9

> P117. 'Ermanox 4.5 * 6 cm' ... The classic V.P.camera made famous by the photographers who used it. Erich Salamon's candid pictures of the Nazi party leaders in pre-war Germany taken with the rare f2 lens brought it into prominence. There is also a model with an f1.8 lens. c.1926

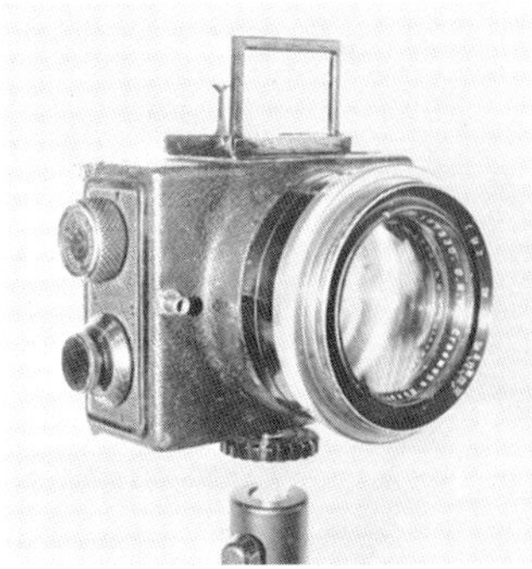

> P119 'Ermanox V.P. Reflex' ... A small V.P. miniature reflex. Based on the Ermanox design (Ref. P117 above) it should not be confused with the smaller 'Ernoflex' which was also made in the V.P. format. The lens was an Ernostar f 1.8 105 mm. in helical focussing mount. c.1926.

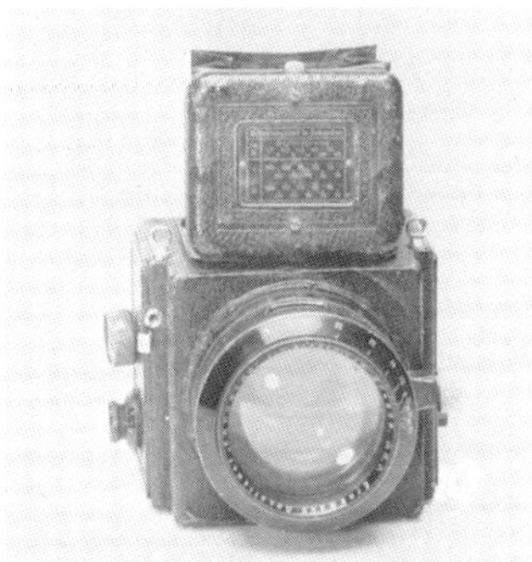

> S13. 'Expo/Ticka' ... The 'Expo' made in New York and the 'Ticka' in London by HOUGHTON were the same camera. They were made in many variations including a Ticka which showed the workings of a clock on the outside. Silver presentation and monogrammed models (e.g S14) are very highly prized.

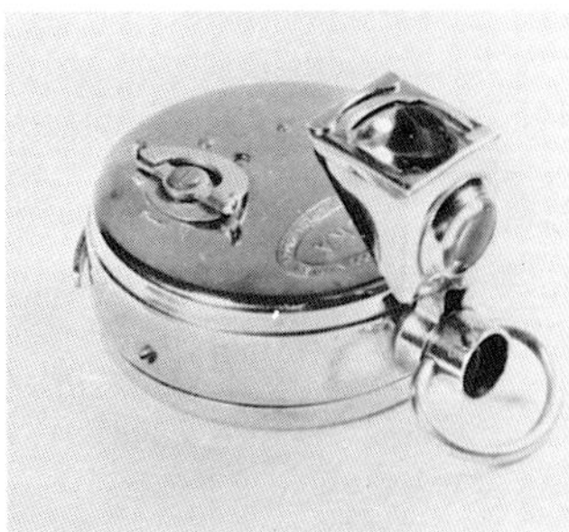

Ref	Name	Data	Average Condition Price Range £	$
FERRO (Italy)				
S16	'GF 82' sub-min. ring camera	*	a. 300	a. 550
FEX (Paris)				
R113	'Fotofex' folding 6.5 * 9 cm.	*	a. 55	a. 95
R114	'Ultrafex' plastic(12 on 120)	pcc	Under 5	Under 9
FOLMER & SCHWING/EKC (New York)				
> P131	'Graflex' S.L.R. (various)	*****	55-60	95-110
P132	'Graflex' 7 * 5 in. outfit	*	a. 190	a. 340
P133	'R.B. Cycle Graphic' outfit	**	220-260	380-460
P134	'Speed Graphic' (various)	****	70-85	120-150
R115	'Cirkut No 5' panoram	**	170-200	280-340
R116	'Cirkut No 6' panoram	**	440-550	800-1000
R117	'Cirkut No 10' panoram	*	a. 600	a. 1100
R118	'Graflex' S.L.R. press	***	75-90	130-160
R119	'No 0 Graphic'	**	90-110	160-200
FOLMER GRAFLEX see GRAFLEX				
FOTET (= KOCHMANN Dresden)				
R120	'Fotet' strut (16 on 127)	*	a. 55	a. 95
FOTH (Berlin)				
R121	'Derby' folding (8 on 127)	**	25-30	45-55
R122	'Derby' with c.r.f.	*	a. 70	a. 120
R123	'Derby' (Elmar lens)	*	a. 140	a. 240
R124	'De Luxe' (alligator skin)	**	35-45	65-80
R125	'Fothflex' T.L.R.	*	a. 50	a. 90
FOTOFEX (Berlin)				
R126	'Visorflex' rf/pl folding	*	a. 55	a. 95
> S17	'Minifex' sub-miniature 16mm	*	a. 180	a. 320
FRANCAIS E (Paris)				
P135	'Kinegraph' T.L.R. 9 * 12 cm	*	a. 500	a. 900
FRANKA (Beyreuth)				
R127	'Bonafix' folding	pcc	5-10	9-18
> R128	'Solida 1/11' (12 on 120)	pcc	5-10	9-18
R129	'Solida 111' (unc. r.f.)	pcc	15-30	25-50
FRANKE & HEIDECKE (Braunschweig)				
P136	'Heidoscop' stereo	**	170-200	280-340
Q101	'Rollei 35' (3.5 Tessar)	***	70-85	120-150
Q102	'Rollei 35B' (3.5 Triotar)	**	35-45	65-80

> P131 'Graflex'

... A long lasting line of American reflex cameras first made by FOLMER & SCHWING then by that division of EKC then by FOLMER-GRAFLEX and GRAFLEX Inc. P131 covers versions in sizes 2 1/4 * 3 1/4 to 7 * 5 in. but excludes the 'Big Berthas' with long lenses.

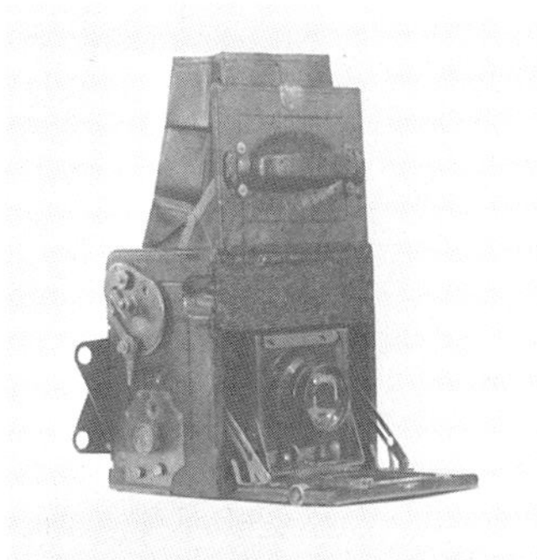

> S17. 'Minifex'

... Designed by Fritz Kaftanski who specialised in sub-miniatures the 'Minifex' was a real camera for 16mm rollfilm. The body is dominated by the shutter in its various versions. Illustrated is the best of them with a Compur shutter. c.1932

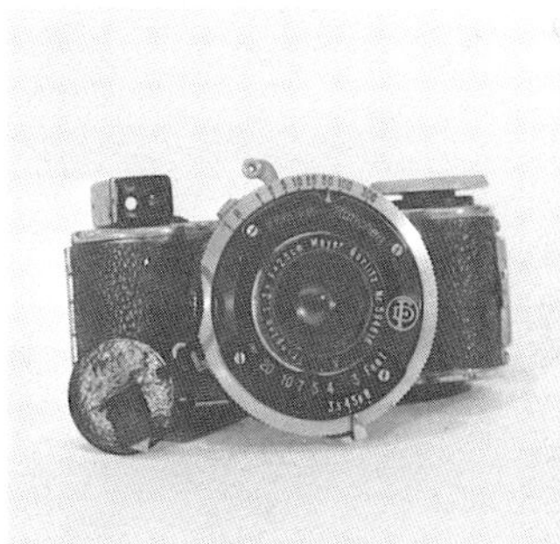

> R128. 'Solida 1 or 11'

... A range of folding bed rollfilm cameras in both vertical and horizontal format started pre-WW2 and continuing until the 1950's. Basically for 12 exposures 6 * 6 cm on 120 film but some models with 4 * 4 cm mask. Various lens and shutter combinations.

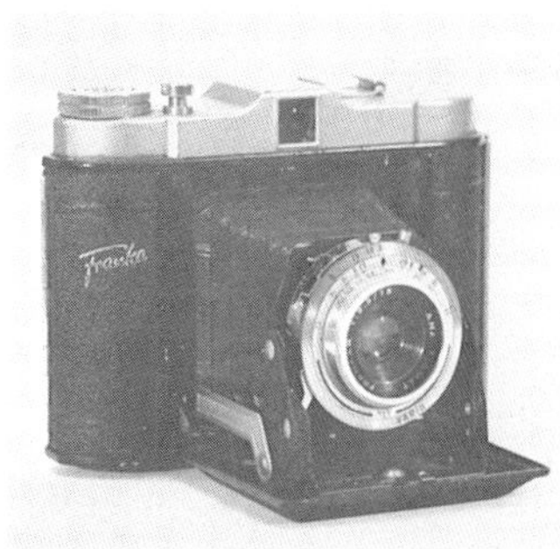

FRANKE & HEIDECKE (Braunschweig)(cont'd)

Ref	Name	Data	Average Condition Price Range £	$
Q103	'Rollei 35S' (f2 Sonnar)	**	70-85	120-150
Q104	'Rollei 35S' (60 Annivers'y)	*	a. 280	a. 500
Q105	'Rollei SL35'	*	a. 50	a. 90
R130	'Rolleidoscop' stereo reflex	***	460-550	800-1000
> R131	'Rolleicord 1'(f4.5 Triotar)	*****	65-75	120-140
R132	'Rolleicord 1/1a'(f3.8Triotar)	***	35-45	65-80
R133	'Rolleicord 1a (f4.5 Triotar)	***	25-30	45-55
R134	'Rolleicord 11 or 11a'	***	40-50	70-85
R135	'Rolleicord 111 or 1V'	***	40-50	70-85
R136	'Rolleicord Va/Vb'(f3.5 Xenar)	****	55-65	95-120
R137	'Rolleicord Vb' outfit	*	a. 260	a. 460
> R138	'Rolleiflex 1' (original)	****	55-65	95-120
R139	'Rolleiflex Old Standard'	****	45-55	80-95
R140	'Rolleiflex New Standard'	****	30-35	50-60
R141	'Rolleiflex Automat'	****	55-65	95-120
R142	'Rolleiflex 2.8a'	*	a. 40	a. 70
R143	'Rolleiflex 2.8d or 2.8e'	***	170-200	280-340
R144	'Rolleiflex 3.5e or 3.5f'	****	150-180	260-320
R145	'Rolleiflex 3.5e' outfit	**	260-320	460-550
R146	'Rolleiflex 2.8f'	*	a. 280	a. 500
R147	'Rolleiflex 2.8 (Aurum)'	**	800-1000	1400-1700
R148	'Rolleiflex MX'	*	a. 55	a. 95
R149	'Rolleiflex T' (grey/black)	****	140-170	240-300
R150	'Rolleiflex 4*4' (Grey Baby)	****	80-100	140-170
R151	'Rolleiflex 4*4' in makers box	*	a. 180	a. 320
R152	'Rolleiflex 4*4' (Sports)	***	100-120	170-200
R153	'Rolleiflex 4*4' (Original)	**	60-75	110-130
R154	'Rolleimagic' (f3.5 Xenar)	***	100-120	170-200
R155	'SL 66 ME' (f2.8 Planar)	*	a. 380	a. 650
R156	'Tele-Rolleiflex'	**	400-480	700-850
> R157	'Wide-Angle Rolleiflex'	**	900-1100	1600-2000
R158	'Rollei 110'	pcc	10-20	18-35
FUJI PHOTO FILM (Japan)				
Q106	'Fujica' S.L.R.	*	a. 30	a. 55
Q107	'Fujica Mini'	**	65-80	110-130
Q108	'Fujica ST605' outfit	*	a. 110	a. 190

> R131. 'Rolleicord 1'

... Produced between 1933 and 1936 this was the first of the famous 6 * 6 cm. 'Rolleicord' T.L.R.'s and is easily recognized by the Art-Deco chequer board pattern nickel plated exterior finish. Fitted with Zeiss f4.5 75mm Triotar lens in Compur shutter.

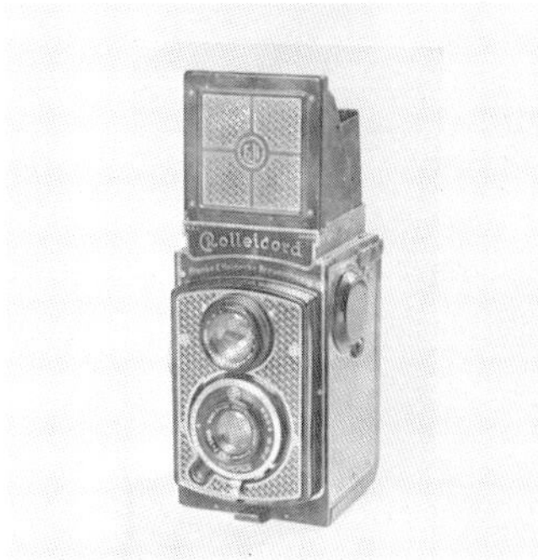

> R138. 'Rolleiflex 1'

... Made in two versions; the first for six exposures on 117 film then for 8 on 120; some of these converted from the earlier type. Both with knob film wind and without exposure counter. Serial numbers below 200,000.
c. 1929 to 1932.

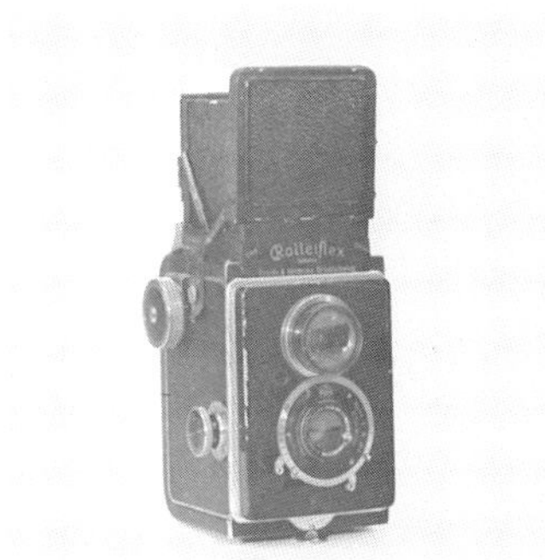

> R157 'Rolleiflex' (W.A)

... Introduced 1961 and made until 1967 in small numbers the Wide-Angle Rolleiflex is comparatively rare and fetches a high price.
It took 12 exposures on 120 film and was fitted with an f4 55mm Distagon in Synchro-Compur shutter.

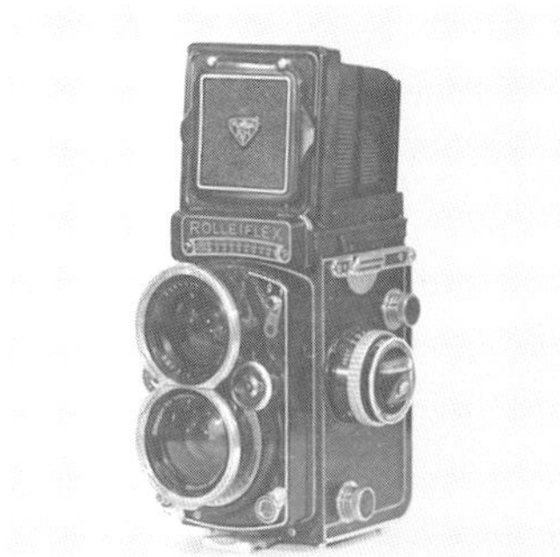

Ref	Name	Data	Average Condition Price Range £	$
FUTURA (Freiberg)				
Q109	'Futura-S' c.r.f	pcc	30-60	55-110
GALLUS (Courbevoie)				
R159	'Derlux' folding V.P.	***	30-35	50-60
GANDOLFI (London)				
> P137	View cameras	****	180-220	320-400
P138	View camera outfits	***	380-460	650-800
P139	Wide-angle cameras	**	380-460	650-800
GAUMONT (Paris)				
> P140	'Block-notes' 4.5 * 6 cm.	***	60-75	110-130
P141	'Spido' 1/4 plate	**	50-60	85-100
P142	'Stereo Block-notes' V.P.	**	180-220	320-400
P143	'Stereo Spido'	**	110-130	190-240
GENNERT (New York)				
P144	'Golf Montauk' H & S	*	a. 40	a. 70
GAEVERT (Belgium)				
R161	'Gaevabox 127' brown bakelite	*	a. 12	a. 20
GIBSON (Hull)				
P145	Stereo tailboard 1/2 pl	*	a. 360	a. 650
GNOME (London)				
R162	'Pixie de luxe' box	pcc	5-10	9-18
R163	'Pixieflex' TLR style box	pcc	8-15	13-25
GOERZ (Berlin)				
P146	'Anshutz' press	****	45-55	80-100
P147	'Anshutz' tropical	**	130-160	220-260
P148	Folding reflex 5 * 4 in	*	a. 60	a. 110
P149	'Stereo Anschutz'	***	120-150	220-260
P150	'Stereo Photo Binocle'	*	a. 1000	a. 1800
P151	Tailboard 1/2 pl	*	a. 95	a. 170
R164	Folding rollfilm	pcc	8-15	13-25
GOERZ (Vienna)				
> S18	'Minicord' T.L.R. 16mm	***	120-150	220-260
GOERZ/ZEISS IKON (Germany)				
P152	'Stereo Tenax' 45 * 107 mm	**	90-110	150-180

> P137. 'Gandolfi'

... This London family business concentrated on making high class wood and brass cameras from c.1885 to 1985. All types and sizes were made and are often usable as well as collectable.
A tailboard is illustrated as an example.

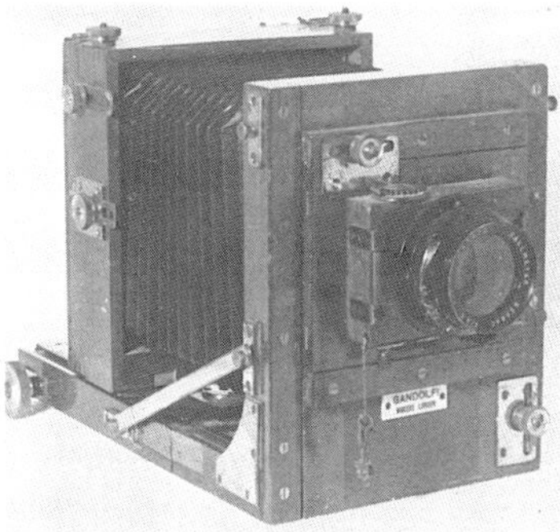

> P140. 'Blocknotes'

... Made in France c.1902 by GAUMONT et Cie the Blocknotes was the first V.P plate camera to sell in quantity.
Focussing is carried out by moving the focal plane and not the lens. The shutter is cocked by erecting the view finder.

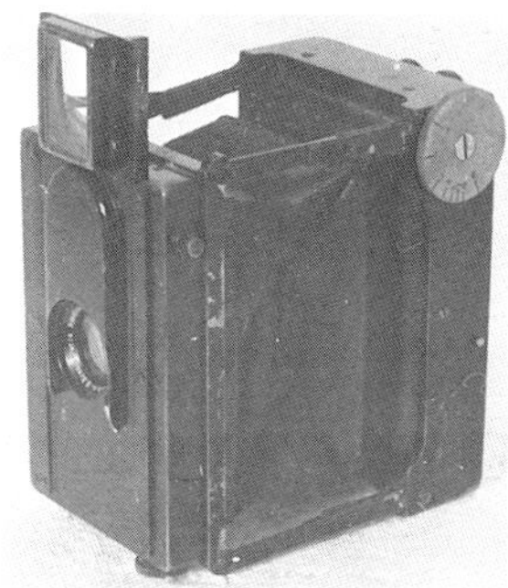

> S18. 'Minicord'

... This precision T.L.R. for 16mm film in special cassettes was made in Austria c.1951.
The front of the camera containing the lens doubled as the projection section for the enlarger which came as part of an outfit.

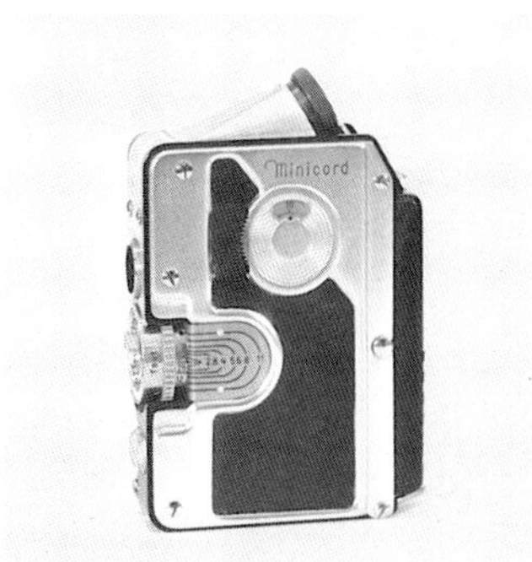

Ref	Name	Data	Average Condition Price Range £	$
GOERZ/ZEISS IKON (Germany)				
P153	'Tenax' folding 1/4 plate	*	a. 40	a. 70
P154	'Tenax' folding pl Tropical	**	260-320	460-550
P155	'Tenax' coat-pocket strut	*	a. 45	a. 80
> P156	'Tenax' vest-pocket strut	***	80-100	140-170
R165	'Roll Tenax' 6 * 9 cm	pcc	10-20	18-35
R166	'Roll Tenax' 4.5 * 6 cm	**	35-45	65-80
GOLDAMMER (Frankfurt)				
R167	'Goldeck' 12 on 120	pcc	8-15	13-25
R168	'Gugo' 12 on 120	pcc	5-10	9-18
GOLDMANN (Vienna)				
P157	Strut Anschutz type 9 * 12 cm	*	a. 60	a. 110
GOLTZ & BREUTMANN (Dresden)				
P158	'Mentor' reflex 9 * 12 cm	***	50-60	85-100
P159	'Mentor' reflex 6.5 * 9 cm.	**	200-240	340-420
P160	'Mentor' Compur reflex	****	75-90	130-160
> P161	'Mentor' folding reflex	**	90-110	160-200
P162	'Mentor' stereo reflex	**	220-260	380-460
GOMZ (Leningrad) also see page 76				
Q111	'Cnopm (Sport)' 50 exposure	*	a. 260	a. 460
Q112	'Cueria-4' (plastic folding)	pcc	8-15	13-25
Q113	'Leningrad' (motorised)	**	70-85	120-150
GOTZ J.R (London)				
P163	Field 1/2 plate	*	a. 100	a. 180
GRAFLEX (New York)				
Q114	'Graphic Century 35' c.r.f.	pcc	15-30	25-50
GRIFFIN (London)				
P164	'Pocket Cyko'	***	200-240	340-420
GRIFFITHS (Birmingham)				
P165	Cardboard detective	*	a. 35	a. 60
GUNDLACH OPTICAL (New York)				
P166	'Korona' H & S 5 * 4 in.	*	a. 60	a. 110
P167	'Korona' pan. view 8 * 20 in	*	a. 550	a. 950
HAKING (Hong Kong)				
Q115	'Halina Paulette'	pcc	5-10	9-18
R169	'Halina' T.L.R. style	pcc	8-15	13-25

> P156 'Tenax V.P.'
... 'Tenax' was the name given to various GOERZ and ZEISS IKON cameras. P156 covers the flat V.P. strut pocket cameras which were fitted with a range of lenses; early ones in guillotine shutters later ones in Compurs.
In production 1910 to 1928.

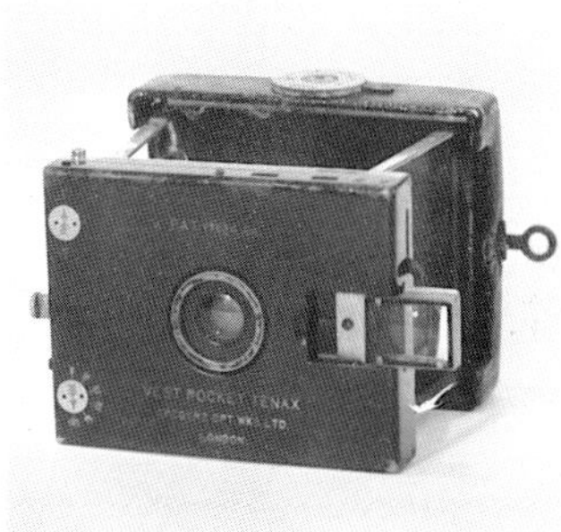

> P160. 'Mentor' Compur SLR
... This is really a plate box camera converted into a single lens reflex. The outstanding feature is the large Compur shutter on the front carrying the Tessar lens. c.1928
Format 9 * 6.5 cm.

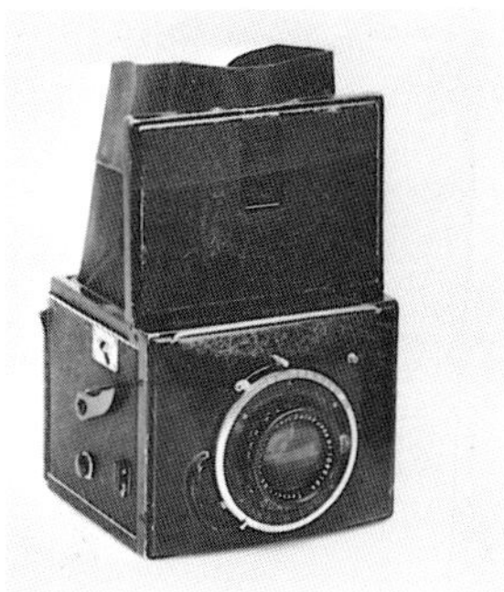

Wanted

I am still looking for a number of single lens reflexes, particularly:
Adams Videx 1908, Radex, BCM Duoflex, Exakta below s/n 400040, Exakta 66 (1950), Gamma Duflex, Miranda by Orion, Lancaster with multislit shutter, unusual folding reflexes, prewar Japanese, larger than 1/2 plate or pre 1900. Also cameras with patent 190302/21, prototypes, rollfilm Palmos, Kirn sub-miniature and rare and unusual lenses. Please write to Stein Falchenberg, Teamwork, 11 Shelton St, London WC2H 9JN

Ref	Name	Data	Average Condition Price Range £	$
HANAU (Paris)				
P168	'Le Marsouin' stereo 45 * 107	*	a. 110	a. 190
HANEEL (Canada)				
Q116	'Tri-Vision Stereo'	*	a. 60	a. 110
HARE GEORGE (London)				
P169	Field cameras	**	110-130	190-240
P170	Tailboard 5 * 7 in.	**	120-150	220-260
P171	Tailboard 1/4 plate outfit	*	a. 400	a. 700
P172	Tailboard 1/1 plate	***	70-85	120-150
P173	Tailboard 10 * 12 in.	*	a. 260	a. 460
P174	Studio camera with stand	*	a. 650	a. 1100
> S19	Changing box	**	55-65	95-120
HASSELBLAD (Sweden)				
> P175	'Svenska Express' falling pl	*	a. 440	a. 750
R170	S.L.R. '500C'	***	550-650	950-1200
R171	S.L.R. '1000F' or '1600F'	***	360-440	650-800
R172	'Superwide' S.L.R.	*	a. 300	a. 550
HAVISTOCK Mfg (London)				
P176	Tailboard 12 * 10 in.	*	a. 100	a. 180
HENRY P (Paris)				
P177	View camera 30 * 25 cm.	*	a. 150	a. 260
HERBERT GEORGE (Chicago)				
R173	'Imperial Debonair' bakelite	pcc	5-10	9-18
HERMAGIS (Paris)				
P178	'Velocigraphe' falling plate	**	240-300	420-500
HILGER (London)				
P179	Spectroscope camera 1/4 plate	*	a. 120	a. 220
HILL G (Birmingham)				
P180	Field 1/2 plate	*	a. 100	a. 180
HOBBIES Ltd (London)				
P181	Field 1/2 plate	**	50-60	85-100
HONG KONG (Maker unknown)				
R174	'Empire' box	pcc	Under 5	Under 9
R175	'Kingston' T.L.R. style	pcc	5-10	9-18
> R176	Plastic novelty cameras	pcc	Under 5	Under 9

> S19. Changing Box

... GEORGE HARE's 'Patent Automatic Changing Box' of 1875 was the first popular automatic box. It took 12 plates and was made in several sizes to match the choice of camera. It was used with special plate holders to transfer plates from holder to box.

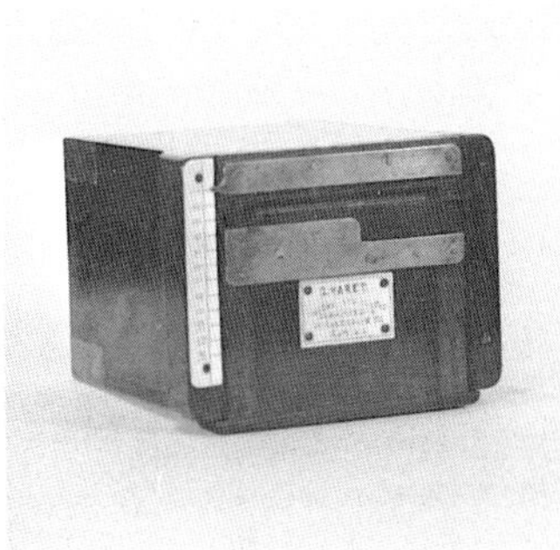

> P175. 'Svenska Express'

... Made c.1910 the merit of this falling plate camera lies in the name HASSELBLAD. Long before Victor made his world famous S.L.R.'s his father ran a trading company in Stockholm and the 'Svenska Express' was sold by the photographic department of that organisation.

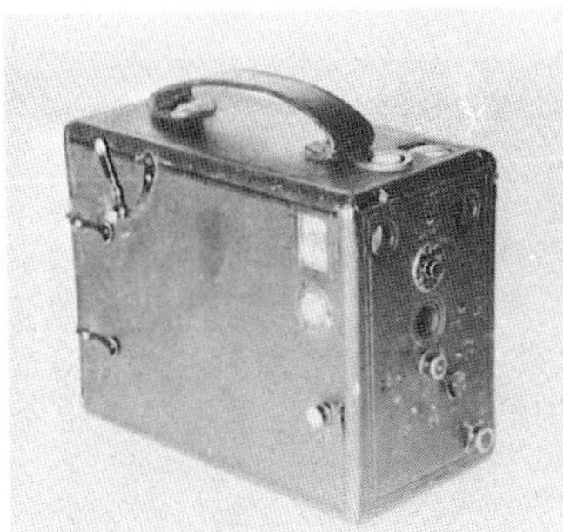

> R176. Novelty Cameras

... This category covers a series of plastic novelty cameras taking 126 size cartridges. The front of the camera is in the shape of a characters head with the lens set in the mouth. Often used for cartoon characters such as Yogi Bear or Fred Flintstone.

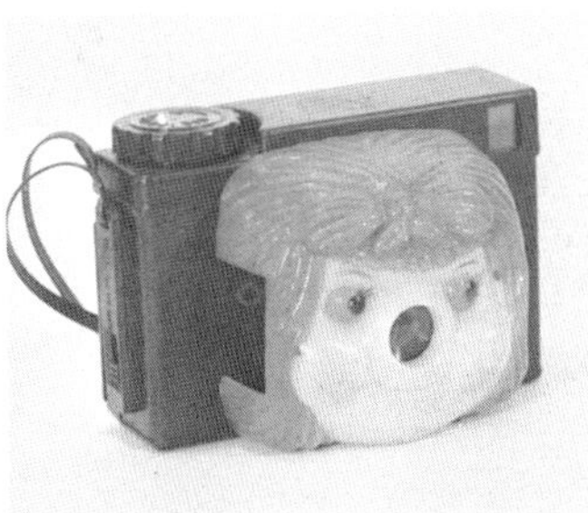

HORNE & THORNTHWAITE (England)(cont'd)

Ref	Name	Data	Average Condition Price Range £	$
P182	Collapsible wet plate	*	a. 2200	a. 3900
P183	Sliding box wet plate	**	700-850	1200-1500
HOUGHTON/H.B.M (London)				
P184	'Cameo' folding plate	**	25-30	45-55
P185	'Ensign' folding 1/4 pl	pcc	15-30	25-50
> P186	'Ensign' S.L.R.	***	35-45	65-80
P187	'Ensign' S.L.R tropical	**	200-240	340-420
P188	'Ensign Tudor' 1/4pl folding	**	20-25	35-45
P189	'Ensign' 1/2 pl field	***	100-120	170-200
P190	'Holborn' (Ilex) falling pl.	***	50-60	85-100
P191	'Holborn' stamp (9 exposure)	***	100-120	170-200
P192	'Klito' (non-focus) fall. pl.	pcc	8-15	13-25
P193	'Klito' (focussing) fall. pl.	pcc	15-30	25-50
P194	'Klito' No 6 falling plate	*	a. 55	a. 95
P195	'Klito' folding 1/4 pl	pcc	10-20	18-35
P196	'Mascot DB3' falling plate	*	a. 20	a. 35
> P197	'Royal Mail' (15 exposure)	***	460-550	800-1000
P198	'Sanderson' field 1/2 pl.	****	110-130	200-240
P199	'Sanderson' field 1/1 pl.	***	120-150	220-260
P200	'Sanderson' field 10 * 8 in	**	160-200	280-340
P201	'Sanderson' field tropical	*	a. 280	a. 500
> P202	'Sanderson' H & S 1/4 plate	*****	95-100	160-180
P203	'Sanderson' H & S 1/2 plate	***	100-120	170-200
P204	'Sanderson' H & S de-luxe	*	a. 280	a. 500
P205	'Sanderson' H & S tropical	****	280-340	480-600
P206	'Shuttle' falling plate	**	85-100	140-170
P207	Stereo falling plate	*	a. 150	a. 260
P208	'Stereolette' boxform	**	340-420	600-750
P209	Studio 1/2 plate	**	80-100	140-170
P210	Studio tailboard 15 * 12 in	*	a. 220	a. 380
P211	'The Automatic' detective	*	a. 240	a. 420
P212	'The Ensign Sanderson' 1/4 pl	*	a. 280	a. 500
P213	'Triad' 1/4 plate	*	a. 500	a. 900
P214	'Triple Victo' field 1/2 pl	***	100-120	170-200
P215	'Victo' field 1/2 plate	***	70-85	120-150
R177	'Ensign All-Distance Box'	pcc	Under 5	Under 9

> P186. 'Ensign' S.L.R.
... An orthodox design S.L.R. for plates made in a range of sizes from 1/2 pl to 3 1/4 * 2 1/4 in. This robustly designed camera continued in production from c.1908 to c.1935 as the 'Popular Reflex' the 'Deluxe Reflex' and the 'Special Reflex' etc.

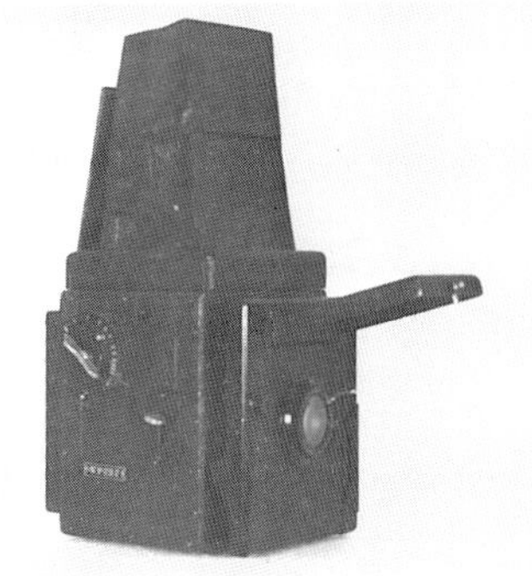

> P197. 'Royal Mail'
... This is one version by HOUGHTON's of the so called 'stamp cameras' which were used to take a set of head and shoulder portraits by multiple exposure. A set of prints framed to look like a sheet of postage stamps was produced. The 'Royal Mail' took 15 exposures. c.1910.

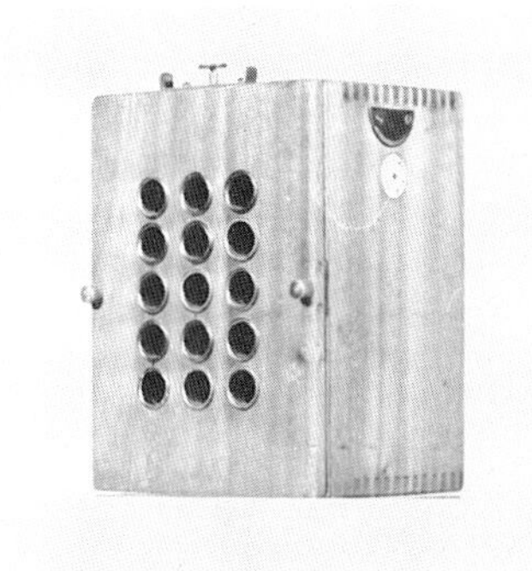

> P202. 'Sanderson H & S'
... One of the most long lived of named plate cameras starting in production in 1899 and continuing in one or more of its many forms until 1940. Most common is the 1/4 plate size. This versatile design was (and still is) a very usable large format camera.

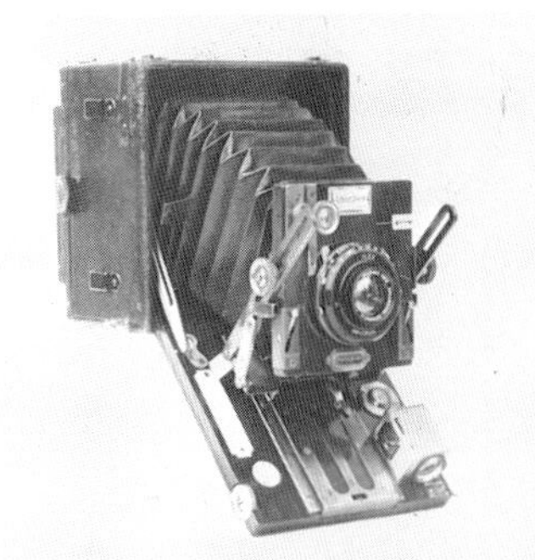

HOUGHTON/H.B.M (London)(cont'd)

Ref	Name	Data	Average Condition Price Range £	$
R178	'Ensign Autorange' c.r.f.	***	30-35	50-60
R179	'Ensign Autospeed'	**	65-80	110-130
R180	'Ensign Cadet' box	pcc	5-10	9-18
R181	'Ensign Carbine No ..	pcc	8-15	13-25
> R182	'Ensign Carbine' tropical	****	50-60	90-110
R183	'Ensign Commando' c.r.f.	**	25-30	45-55
R184	'Ensign Cupid'(T-shape body)	pcc	15-30	25-50
R185	'Ensign Double Eight'	**	25-30	45-55
R186	'Ensign E29 box' (blue)	pcc	8-15	13-25
R187	'Ensign Folding'(early types)	pcc	8-15	13-25
R188	'Ensign Fulvue' (black)	pcc	5-10	9-18
R189	'Ensign Greyhound' folding	pcc	8-15	13-25
R190	'Mayfair' box	pcc	5-10	9-18
R191	'Ensign Mickey Mouse'	**	35-45	65-80
R192	'Ensign Multex' c.r.f	*	a. 100	a. 180
> R193	'Ensign Midget' compact	**	25-30	45-55
R194	'Ensign Pocket 20'	pcc	5-10	9-18
R195	'Ensign Ranger' folding	pcc	8-15	13-25
R196	'Ensign Ranger Special'	pcc	10-20	18-35
> R197	'Ensign Rollfilm Reflex'	***	35-45	65-80
R198	'Ensign Reflex' tropical	***	220-260	380-460
R199	'Ensign Selfix' (art-deco)	pcc	15-30	25-50
R200	'Ensign Selfix' (Xpres)	pcc	15-30	25-50
R201	'Ensign Selfix' (Ensar)	pcc	8-15	13-25
R202	'Ensign Selfix' (Rosstar)	pcc	10-20	18-35
R203	'Ensign Selfix Special'	**	25-30	45-55
R204	'Ensign Snapper' folding	pcc	5-10	9-18
R205	'Ensign' folding V.P.	*	a. 17	a. 30
R206	'G28' aircraft gun outfit	*	a. 650	a. 1100
R207	'Nos 1 or 2 Ensignette'	***	25-30	45-55
R208	'No 2 Ensignette' de luxe	*	a. 80	a. 140
R209	'No 2 Ensignette' (plated)	*	a. 100	a. 180
R210	'Sanderson' H & S (rollfilm)	**	70-85	120-150
HUNTER R.F (London)				
R211	'Gilbert' box	pcc	10-20	18-35

> R182. Tropical Carbine
... Originally made in four models it later became the 'Ensign Tropical 20'. This folding camera was made in brass finished in Florentine Bronze with tan bellows. First fitted c.1920's with f4.5 Tessar in Compur later with an Ensar lens in Prontor or Mulchro shutter.

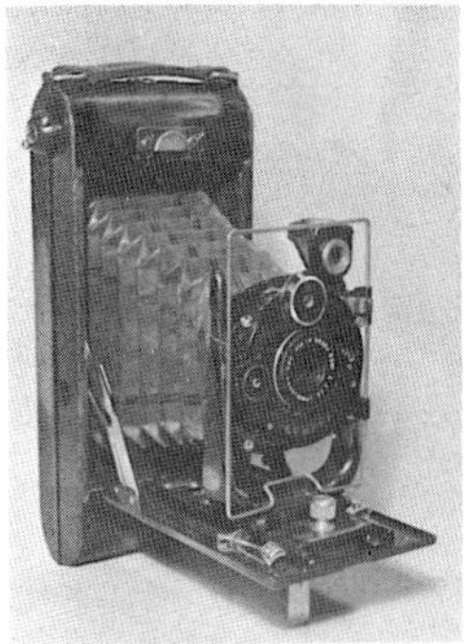

> R193. 'Ensign Midget'
...A 1927-1937 camera taking 6 exposures 3 * 4 cm. on special film. R193 covers the three models (as priced in shillings); the '22' with simple shutter; the '33' with three speed shutter and the '55' with f6.3 Ensar lens. The Silver Jubilee models are not included.

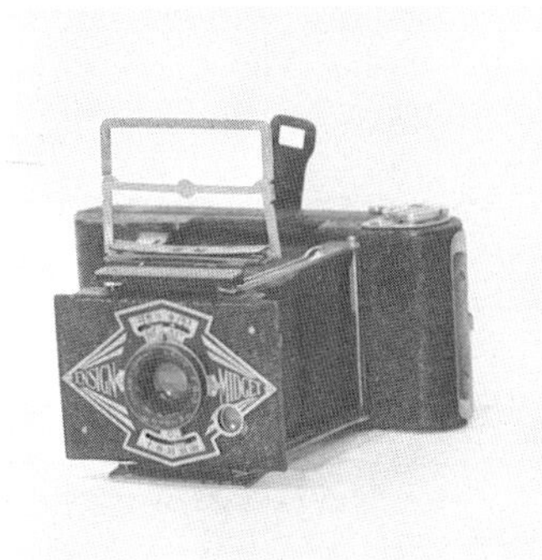

> R197. 'Ensign R.F. Reflex'
... This category combines the 'Ensign Roll Film Reflex' with front shutter the 'Focal Plane' and the 'Speed' and 'Carbine' Roll Film Reflexes. All were for 8 exposures on 120 film (3 1/4 * 2 1/4 in.). Standard lenses were the f7.7 Aldis or f4.5 Ensar.c.1920's/30's.

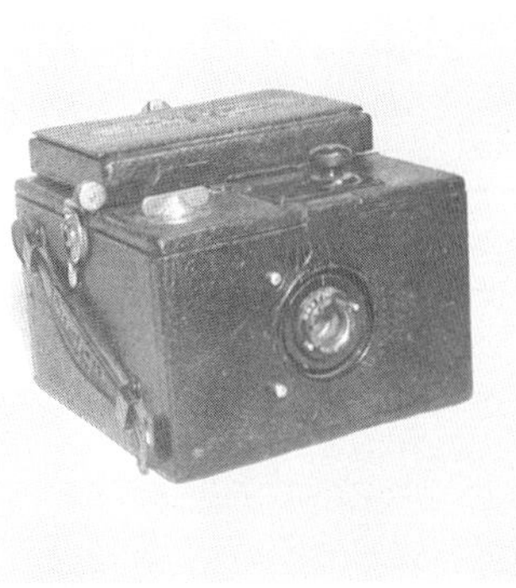

Ref	Name	Data	Average Condition Price Range £	$
HURTER & DRIFFIELD (London)				
S20	'Actinograph' exposure meter	**	110-130	190-240
HUTTIG (Dresden)				
P216	Boxform reflex 9 * 12 cm.	*	a. 220	a. 380
ICA (Dresden) also see page 108				
P217	'Atom' 4.5 * 6 cm	**	95-120	170-200
P218	Single Lens Reflex	*	a. 40	a. 70
P219	Tropical folding 15 * 10 cm	*	a. 95	a. 170
R212	Aircraft camera 13 * 18 cm.	*	a. 70	a. 120
R213	'Carbine' (rollfilm)	**	30-35	50-60
ICA/ZEISS IKON (Germany)				
> P220	'Bebe' 4.5 * 6 cm	**	130-160	220-260
P221	'Bebe' 6.5 * 9 cm	**	60-75	110-130
P222	'Favorit' fold.trop.9 * 12 cm	*	a. 180	a. 320
P223	Folding V.P.	*	a. 100	a. 180
P224	'Ideal' folding 9 * 12 cm.	**	25-30	45-55
P225	'Nixe 555' 9 * 12 cm folding	**	25-30	45-55
P226	'Plaskop' stereo boxform	*	a. 40	a. 70
P227	'Polyscop' stereo 45 * 107 mm	****	110-130	190-220
P228	'Stereo Ideal'	**	140-170	240-300
P229	'Trona' folding 9 * 12 cm	*	a. 25	a. 45
P230	'Volta' 9 * 12 cm folding	**	25-30	45-55
R214	'Icarette' 6 * 9 cm (120)	**	25-30	45-55
R215	'Icarette' 6 * 6 cm (117)	pcc	30-60	55-110
R216	'Nixe 595' (rollfilm/plate)	**	25-30	45-55
R217	'Plascop Stereo'	*	a. 65	a. 110
IHAGEE (Dresden)				
P231	'Duplex'	**	20-25	35-45
P232	Folding plate 6.5 * 9 cm	pcc	20-40	35-70
> P233	Folding reflex 6.5 * 9 cm	*	a. 130	a. 220
P234	Strut focal plane 6.5 * 9 cm	*	a. 60	a. 110
Q117	'Exa 1 and 1a' S.L.R.	pcc	15-30	25-50
Q118	'Exa 11 11a or 500' S.L.R.	**	25-30	45-55
> Q119	'Exakta' S.L.R's (Varex etc)	***	40-50	70-85
Q120	'Exakta' S.L.R. outfits	***	90-100	160-200
Q121	'Kine-Exakta' (original)	*	a. 650	a. 1100
Q122	'Kine Exakta 1 & 11'	**	65-80	110-130

> P202. ICA 'Bebe' V.P.
... This strut type V.P. plate camera had a long life originating with ZULAUF (Ref P493) then with ICA and finally ZEISS IKON. The f4.5 Tessar lens and Compur shutter were built into a flat housing attached to a substantial helical screw for focussing. 1905 to 1923.

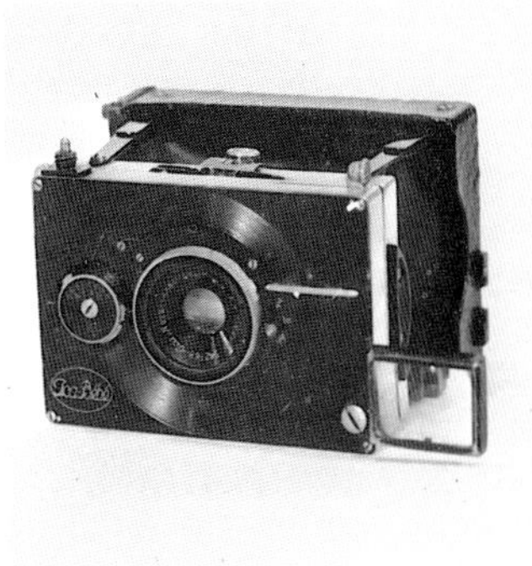

> P233. Folding Reflex
... This can be regarded as one of the more successful attempts to design a compact plate S.L.R. as it folded into an easily opened (and closed) flat package. Most models are in the 6.5 * 9 cm. size but also made as a 9 * 12 cm. camera. c.1924.

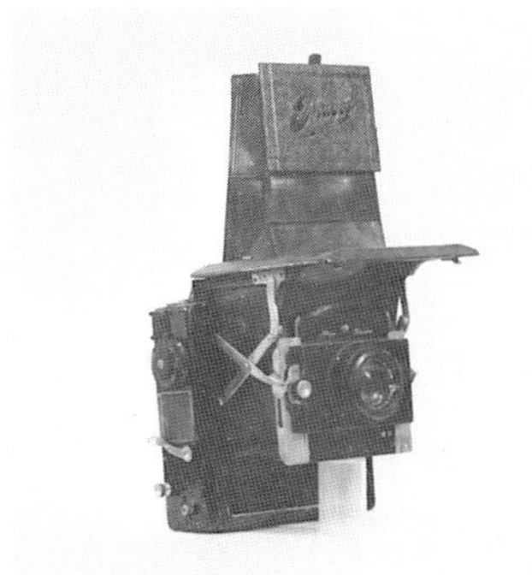

> Q119. 'Exakta' S.L.R.
... This category covers all 35 mm Exakta's except the 1936 to 1946 Kine Exakta's. It includes the the 'Varex' 'VX' and the 'V' models.
The collectors price tends to be more dependant upon condition and fitments than on the particular model.

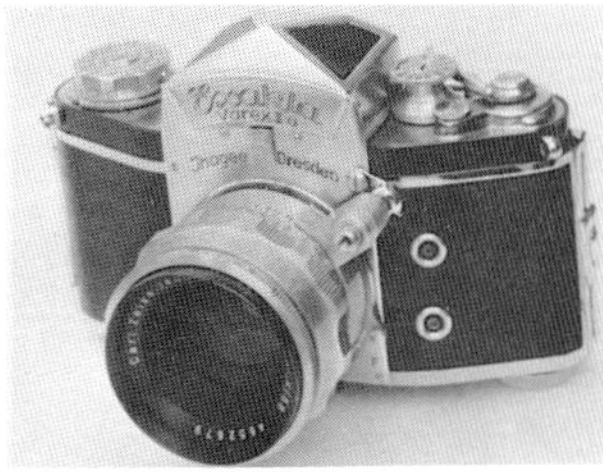

IHAGEE (Dresden)(cont'd)

Ref	Name	Data	Average Condition Price Range £	$
Q123	'Kine Exakta' military	*	a. 100	a. 180
R218	Folding rollfilm	pcc	8-15	13-25
R219	'Exakta V.P.' S.L.R	****	65-80	120-140
R220	'Exakta V.P. Junior'	**	45-55	80-100
R221	'Exakta 66' S.L.R.	**	240-300	420-500
R222	'Night Exakta' S.L.R.	**	240-300	420-500
R223	'Parvola' or 'Baby Ultrix'	***	25-30	45-55
R224	'Ultrix' stereo	***	75-90	130-160
ILFORD (London)				
Q124	'Advocate' (white enamelled)	***	25-30	45-55
> Q125	'Sportsman' (made by DACORA)	pcc	5-10	9-18
Q126	'Witness' c.r.f.	***	360-440	650-800
R225	'Craftsman' T.L.R..style	pcc	5-10	9-18
R226	'Envoy' box	pcc	5-10	9-18
R227	'Sporti'/'Super Sporti'	pcc	Under 5	Under 9
R228	'Sprite' grey plastic	pcc	Under 5	Under 9
IMPERIAL DRY PLATE (England)				
S21	'Imperial' exposure meters	pcc	5-10	9-18
ISO (Milan)				
> R229	'Duplex Super' mono/stereo	**	70-85	120-150
JANOVITCH (London)				
> S22	'Jano' ferrotype camera	**	40-50	70-85
S221	'While-you-Wait' camera	**	40-50	70-85
JAPANESE (Maker unknown)				
S23	'Hit' novelty cameras 16mm	**	14-17	25-30
JAPY (France)				
R231	'Le Pascal'motorized boxform	**	140-170	240-300
JEANNERET/LEIBE (Paris)				
P236	'Monobloc' stereo 45 * 107 mm	***	100-120	170-200
JOS-PE (Hamburg)				
P237	Three colour one-shot V.P.	*	a. 850	a. 1500
JONTE (Paris)				
P238	Tailboard 9 * 12 cm.	*	a. 45	a. 80
JOUX (Paris)				
P239	Stereo jumelle	*	a. 120	a. 220

> Q125. 'Sportsman'
... 1960's. ILFORD version of the DACORA 'Dignette'. A rigid body non-rangefinder 35 mm camera focussing to one metre; f2.8 45 mm Dacora lens with click stops in 3-speed Prontor shutter X sync; self-resetting counter lever wind; film reminder dial & depth of field scale.

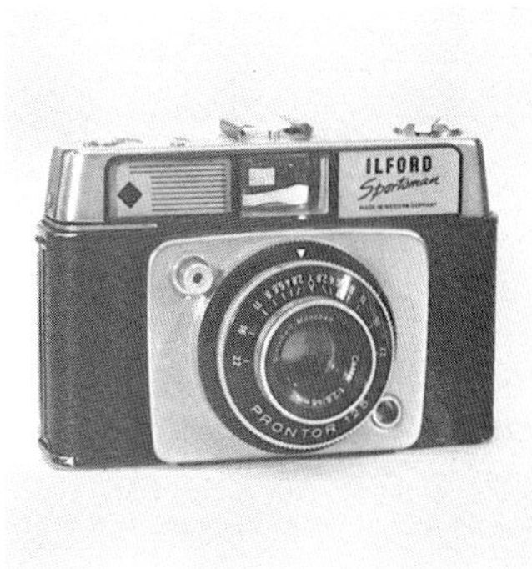

> R229. 'Duplex Super'
... A novel mono or stereo 120 roll film camera c.1956. Stereo pairs 24 * 24 mm were obtained side by side with the film advance operating vertically.
It had a pair of f3.5 35 mm Iriar lenses with common gearing in a five speed shutter.

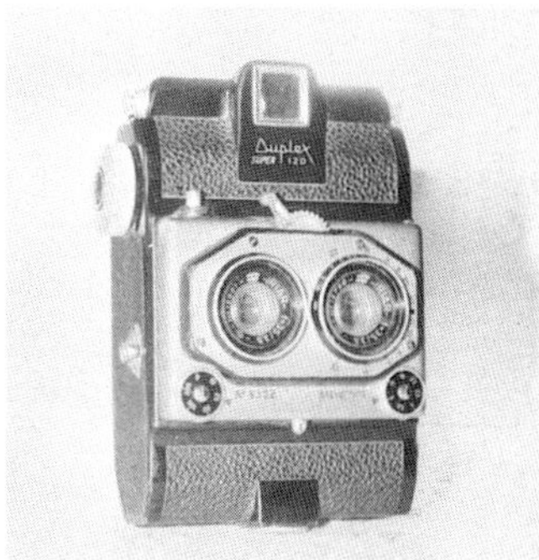

> S22. 'Jano' ferrotype
... This 'while-you-wait' camera is of the same design as the MOORE 'Aptus' (Ref.S44 page 80). It is not known whether the design was copied or purchased by JANOVITCH. It was capable of being loaded with either ferrotype plates or positive cards. c. 1930 to 1950.

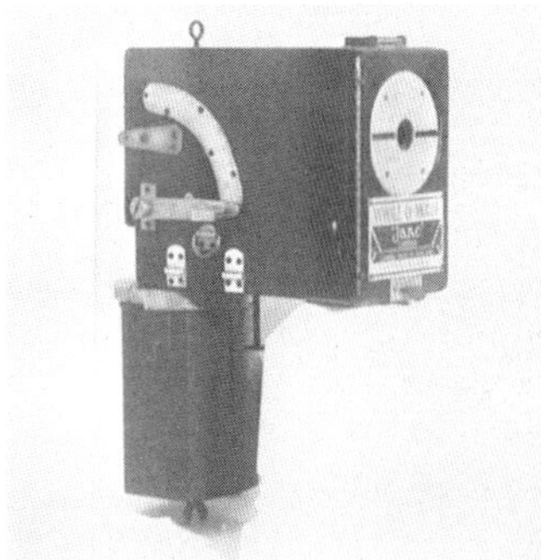

Ref	Name	Data	Average Condition Price Range £	$
JUNKA (Germany)				
R232	'Junka' miniature 3 * 4 cm.	**	25-30	45-55
KAFTANSKI/SIDA (Berlin/London)				
S24	'Sida' 25*25 mm miniature	**	25-30	45-55
KARORAN (Japan)				
R233	'Carperu' (Ikonta copy)	pcc	8-15	13-25
KEMPER (Chicago)				
> S25	'Kombi'miniature camera/viewer	****	140-160	240-280
KENNEDY IND./ILFORD (London)				
> Q127	'K1 Monobar' monorail	**	460-550	800-1000
KERN (Aarau Switzerland)				
P240	'Bijou' Hand & Stand	*	a. 120	a. 220
KERSHAW see APEM				
KINN (France)				
R234	'Kinax 11' (black) folding	pcc	10-20	18-35
R235	'Kinax 111' folding	pcc	20-40	35-70
KINORA (England)				
> S26	Picture Viewer (with rolls)	***	280-340	480-600
KMZ (also see page 100)				
Q128	'Zenit Photo-Sniper'	*	a. 110	a. 190
Q129	'Zenit' S.L.R.	***	18-20	30-35
Q130	'Zorki' Leica copies	***	25-30	45-55
KNIGHT G (London)				
P241	Daguerrotype/wet pl slide box	**	800-1000	1400-1700
KOCHMANN (Dresden)				
P242	'Korelle P' 4.5 * 6 cm.	**	200-240	340-420
Q131	'Korelle K' 1/2 frame	*	a. 110	a. 190
R236	'Reflex Korelle' S.L.R.	***	30-35	50-60
KODAK/EASTMAN (New York etc.)				
P243	Eastman (plate) Nos 3.4.5	***	65-80	110-130
P244	'Specialist' 1/1 or 1/2 pl.	***	65-80	110-130
P245	Studio camera and stand	**	90-110	160-200
P246	Wide angle 1/1 plate	*	a. 75	a. 130
P247	'Zenith' 3 1/4 * 4 1/4 in.	*	a. 160	a. 280
Q132	'Autocolorsnap'	pcc	5-10	9-18
Q133	'Bantam'/'Bantam f8/f6.3'	pcc	8-15	13-25

> S25. 'Kombi'
... An interesting and simple design c.1892 which not only functioned as a camera taking 25 exposures on rollfilm but could also be used as a graphoscope for viewing the finished roll of positives by looking through the lens.
Hence the name 'Kombi'.

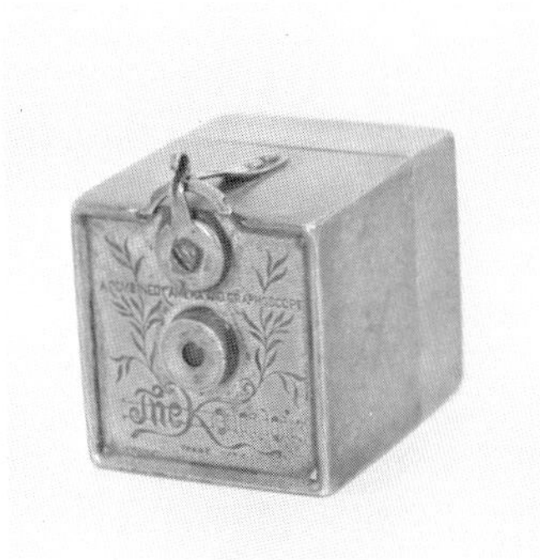

> Q127. 'K1 Monobar'
... A 35 mm technical camera introduced 1962 designed to have all the facilities expected of large format equipment. To quote the Christie catalogue of Jan.1988 'A novel design that ensured few were sold. Finally remaindered at end of 1960's/early 1970's'.

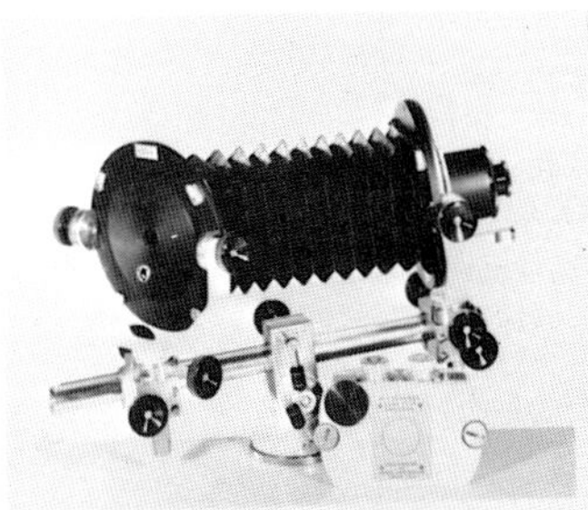

> S26. 'Kinora' viewer
... One example of an apparatus designed to use the persistence of vision phenomena giving the impression of continuous motion from a series of consecutive images. Kinora viewers are particularly sought after when a few rolls are included.

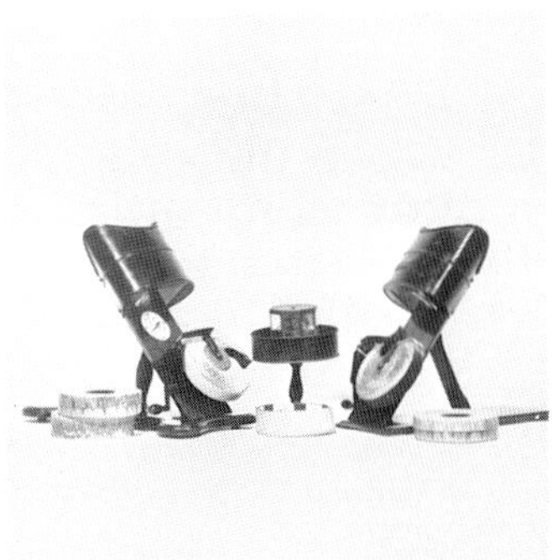

	Ref	Name	Data	Average Condition Price Range £	$
	Q134	'Bantam f4.5/5.6'	pcc	10-20	18-35
	Q135	'Bantam Colorsnap'	pcc	5-10	9-18
>	Q136	'Bantam Special' c.r.f.	***	90-110	160-200
	Q137	'Coloursnap 35'	pcc	5-10	9-18
	Q138	'Ektra 35' c.r.f.	**	240-300	420-500
	Q139	'Motormatic'	**	35-45	65-80
	Q140	'Pony' 35 mm cameras	pcc	8-15	13-25
	Q141	'Kodak 35' (no rangefinder)	pcc	15-30	25-50
	Q142	'Rangefinder 35'	pcc	20-40	35-70
	Q143	'Signet' cameras	pcc	15-30	25-50
	Q144	'Stereo 35'	*	a. 60	a. 110
	R237	'A.K.'(Autographic Kodaks)	pcc	10-20	18-35
	R238	'A.K. Junior'	pcc	8-15	13-25
	R239	'A.K. Special' (not c.r.f)	pcc	10-20	18-35
	R240	'A.K. Special' with c.r.f	*	a. 30	a. 55
	R241	'Baby Brownie'/'B.B.Special'	pcc	5-10	9-18
>	R242	'Beau Brownie' art-deco box	**	25-30	45-55
	R243	'Box Brownie' (original)	**	240-300	420-500
	R244	'Box Brownie' (early type)	**	35-45	65-80
	R245	'Box Brownie' with Pixie box	**	60-75	110-130
	R246	'Box Brownie' (coloured)	pcc	5-10	9-18
	R247	'Box Brownie No 0' (127 film)	pcc	8-15	13-25
	R248	'Box Brownie' (common types)	pcc	Under 5	Under 9
>	R249	'Boy Scout' or 'Girl Guide'	****	90-100	150-170
	R250	'Brownie Autosnap'	pcc	5-10	9-18
	R251	'Brownie Bullseye' (8 on 620)	pcc	5-10	9-18
	R252	'Brownie Cresta' (12 on 120)	pcc	5-10	9-18
	R253	'Brownie Fiesta' (12 on 127)	pcc	5-10	9-18
	R254	'Brownie Flash' (coloured)	pcc	5-10	9-18
	R255	'Brownie Reflex' (T.L.R.style)	pcc	5-10	9-18
	R256	'Brownie Special' (616 or 620)	pcc	5-10	9-18
	R257	'Brownie Star....'(12 on 127)	pcc	8-15	13-25
	R258	'Brownie 44A/B' (12 on 127)	pcc	5-10	9-18
	R259	'Brownie Vecta' (8 on 127)	pcc	5-10	9-18
	R260	'Brownie 127' (8 on 127)	pcc	Under 5	Under 9
	R261	'Bullet' Nos 2 to 4 & special	***	40-50	70-85

> Q136. 'Bantam Special'
... The most advanced of the KODAK cameras designed to use 828 film. It had an Art-Deco styled cast aluminium body of high quality and a c.r.f. with helical focussing f2 Ektar lens in a Compur Rapid (1936 to 1940) or Supermatic (1941 to 1948) shutter.

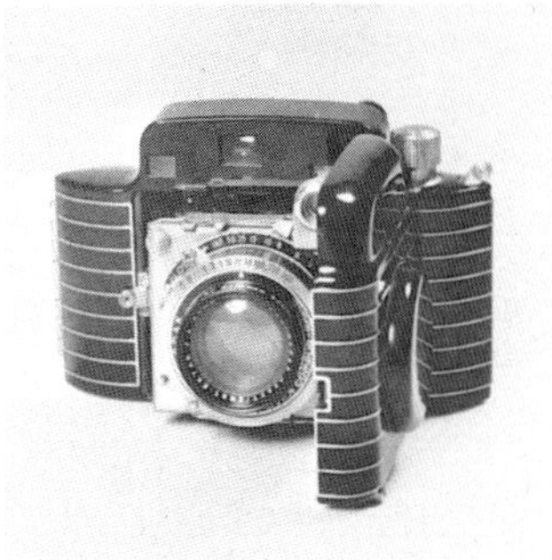

> R242. 'Beau Brownie'
... An Art-Deco box camera made in two sizes :-
3 1/4 * 2 1/4 in. (No 2) or
4 1/4 * 2 1/2 in. (No 2A).
The versions with the faceplate enamelled in black blue or tan sold from 1930 to 1933 and the green and rose faceplate versions from 1930 to 1931.

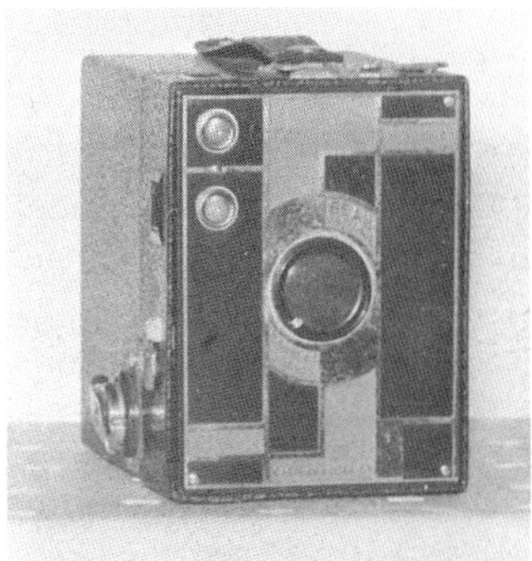

> R249. 'Boy Scout' etc.
... Special variants of the V.P.K. model B were made for the Boy Scout (US & UK) Girl Scout (US) and Girl Guide (UK) movements. Each had the appropriate emblem on the underside of the bed and on the matching case or belt pouch. c.1929 to 1934.

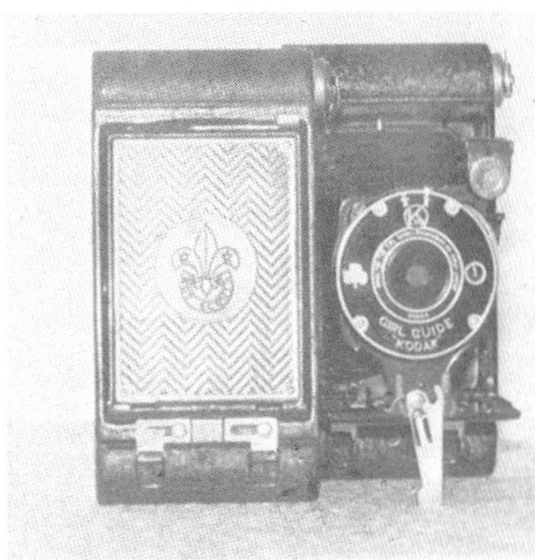

Ref	Name	Data	Average Condition Price Range £	$
> R262	'Bullseye'Nos 2 to 4 & Special	*****	50-55	85-95
R263	'Cartridge Hawkeye' box	pcc	5-10	9-18
R264	'Cartridge Nos 3 & 5'	****	70-85	120-150
R265	'Cartridge No 4'	*****	60-65	100-110
R266	'Chevron' folding (12 on 620)	**	17-20	30-35
R267	'Duaflex' (T.L.R. style)	pcc	5-10	9-18
R268	'Duex'helical focus(8 on 120)	pcc	Under 5	Under 9
R269	Enlarging camera (Jiffy type)	pcc	10-20	18-35
R270	'Falcon' No 2 early boxform	**	40-50	70-85
R271	'Flexo' No 2 early boxform	**	40-50	70-85
R272	'Flushback'(No 3 FPK variant)	**	19-25	35-45
R273	'Folding Autographic Brownie'	pcc	8-15	13-25
R274	'Folding Brownie'(early mods)	pcc	15-30	25-50
R275	'Folding Brownie'(later mods)	pcc	10-20	18-35
R276	'Folding Pocket Brownie'	pcc	10-20	18-35
R277	'Folding Bullseye'	*	a. 95	a. 170
R278	'Folding Hawkeye' (black)	**	17-20	30-35
R279	'Folding Hawkeye' (coloured)	**	25-30	45-55
R280	Folding '66 model 2'	pcc	8-15	13-25
R281	'Folding Kodak No 4A'(1/2pl)	*	a. 70	a. 120
R282	'Folding Kodak Nos 4 and 5'	****	140-170	240-300
R283	'Folding Kodet' roll/plate	**	75-90	130-160
R284	Folding Rollfilm (lots)	*****	10-11	17-19
> R285	'F.P.K. Nos 1/1a' (early)	***	25-30	45-55
R286	'F.P.K. Nos 1/1a' (later)	pcc	8-15	13-25
R287	'F.P.K. No 2' (3 1/2 in sq)	pcc	20-40	35-70
R288	'F.P.K. No 3/3A' (early)	pcc	15-30	25-50
> R289	'F.P.K. Nos 3/3A' (later)	****	18-20	30-35
R290	'F.P.K. No 4' (4 * 5 in.)	***	40-50	70-85
R291	'G24 Gun Camera'	**	35-45	65-80
R292	'Hawkette No 2'bakelite strut	pcc	8-15	13-25
R293	'Hawkeye Ace' or 'Ace de luxe'	pcc	5-10	9-18
R294	'Hawkeye' box (8 on120)	pcc	5-10	9-18
R295	'Holiday Flash' (8 on 127)	pcc	5-10	9-18
R296	'Instamatic Reflex'	pcc	30-60	55-110
R297	'Instamatic 400' (motor wind)	pcc	10-20	18-35

> R262. 'Bullseye'
... Originally made by the BOSTON CAMERA Co. these leather covered box cameras were made between 1896 and 1913. The No2 took 3 1/2 * 3 1/2 in.images on 101 film and the No4 5 * 4 in. on 103 film. The 'Specials' have Rapid Rectilinear lenses instead of Achromatic.

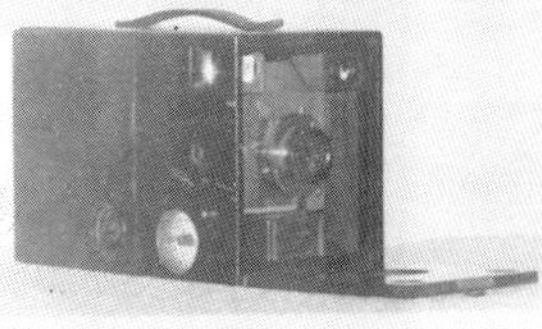

> R285.'F.P.K.No1/1A'(early)
... The original model of 1897 is marked 'Folding Pocket Kodak' without a No; in 1899 it became No1 and the 1A was introduced. These earliest models had no bed and a square front. R285 also includes the second type with bed and self-erecting front.

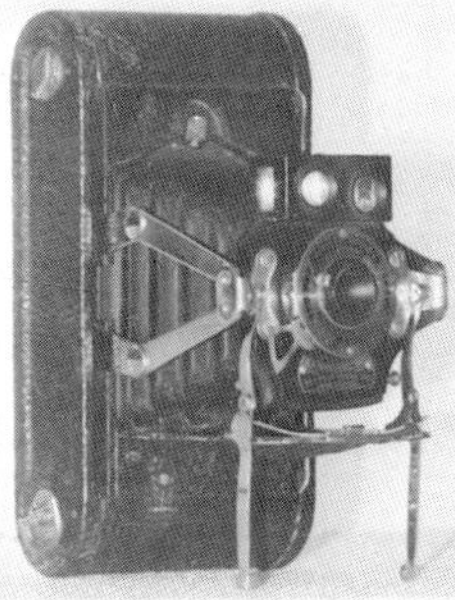

> R289. 'F.P.K. No 3 & 3A'
... This category covers all models of the No 3A and vertically styled bed models of the No 3; both were introduced in 1903 and sold until 1915. Each had several model changes during this time and were fitted with a large number of lens/shutter combinations.

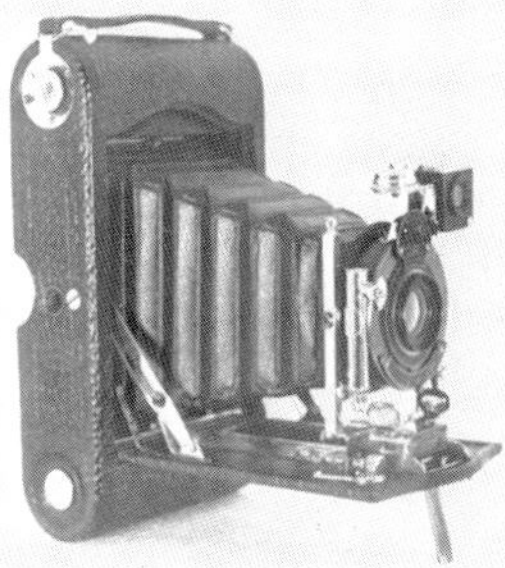

KODAK/EASTMAN (New York etc.)(cont'd)

Ref	Name	Data	Average Condition Price Range £	$
R298	'Instamatic 154' (motor wind)	pcc	15-30	25-50
> R299	'Jiffy Kodak'	pcc	10-20	18-35
R300	'Junior Six-16 and Six-20'	**	17-20	30-35
R301	'K 24' aircraft gun camera'	**	45-55	80-100
R302	'Kodak The' (original model)	***	1000-1200	1700-2100
R303	'Kodet No3' 1/4 plate	*	a. 55	a. 95
R304	'Medalist 1 or 11'	***	90-110	160-200
R305	'Monitor' folding	**	30-35	50-60
R306	'No1/1A Kodak/Kodak Junior'	pcc	5-10	9-18
R307	'No1 Kodak' (factory load)	****	260-320	460-550
R308	'No2 Kodak' (factory load)	**	140-170	240-300
R309	'No3/4 Kodak' (factory load)	****	100-120	170-200
R310	'Ordinary Kodak' model C	*	a. 260	a. 460
R311	'Panoram No 1' 2 1/4 * 7 in.	*****	110-130	200-240
R312	'Panoram No 4' 3 1/2 * 12 in.	****	110-130	190-240
R313	'Petite' (art-deco VPK mod.B)	***	70-85	120-150
R314	'Pocket Kodak No .'(black)	pcc	5-10	9-18
R315	'Pocket Kodak No .'(coloured)	**	30-35	50-60
R316	'Pocket Kodak' (box style)	***	60-75	110-130
R317	'Quick Focus' early boxform	**	70-85	120-150
R318	'Rainbow Hawkeye' coloured	**	30-35	50-60
R319	'Reflex' T.L.R.	**	20-25	35-45
R320	'Screen Focus' (12 on 123)	**	140-170	240-300
> R321	Six-16/20 art-deco folding	pcc	10-20	18-35
R322	'Six-20 Brownie' (folding)	pcc	8-15	13-25
R323	'Six-20 Brownie' (boxes)	pcc	5-10	9-18
R324	'Six-16 Kodak/Kodak Junior'	**	18-20	30-35
R325	'Six-20 Kodak/Kodak Junior'	**	18-20	30-35
R326	'Six-20 Special' bakelite	pcc	5-10	9-18
R327	'Stereo Brownie No 2'	***	160-200	280-340
R328	'Stereo Kodak' folding	**	140-170	240-300
R329	'Sterling 11' folding	pcc	8-15	13-25
R330	'Tourist'folding (8 on 620)	**	18-20	30-35
R331	'Vanity Kodaks' coloured	****	90-110	160-190
R332	'V.P.K.' (lots)	**	5-6	9-11
> R333	'V.P.K.' (type A Autographic)	pcc	8-15	13-25

> R299. 'Jiffy Kodaks'
... A series of Art-Deco strut cameras.
The Six-16 (4 1/4 * 2 1/2 in.on 616 film) 1933 to 1942 and the Six-20 (3 1/4 * 2 1/4 in. on 620 film) 1933 to 1942 had a Twindar lens. The V.P. 'Jiffy' 1935 to 1942 had a fixed focus doublet lens.

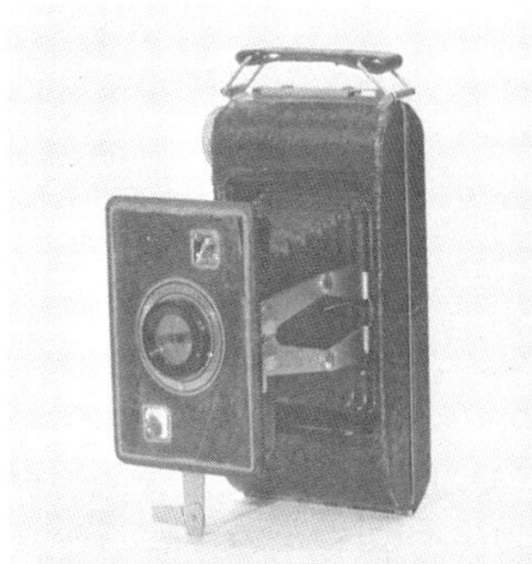

> R321. 'Six-16/20' Art-Deco
... A range of folding cameras inroduced by KODAK with enamelled body sides; rectangular ends and six sided shutter mountings concurrently with the new 616 and 620 films.
c. 1932 to 1937.

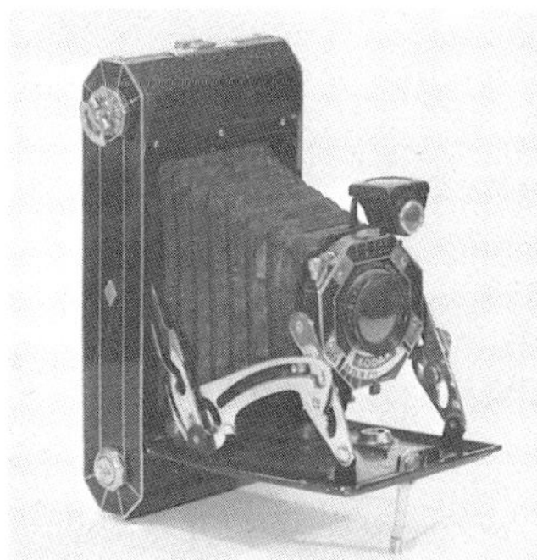

> R333. 'V.P.K.' Type A
... Introduced in 1912 with size 127 rollfilm; side loading with the lens panel supported by trellis struts. R334 covers the 1912 to1914 non-autographic version and R333 the 1915 to 1926 V.P.K. Autographic.
Specials had superior lenses shutters and finish.

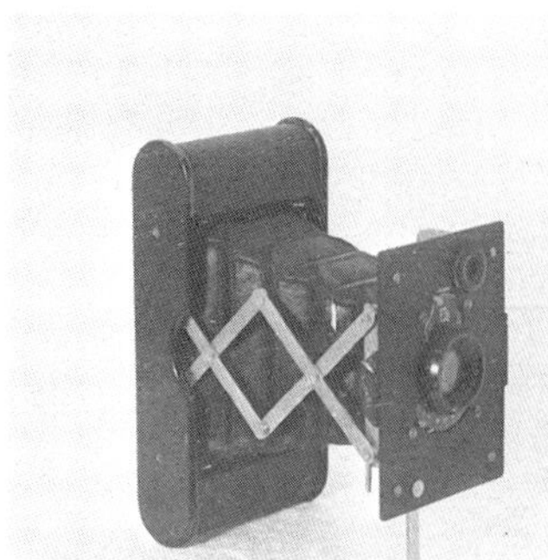

KODAK/EASTMAN (New York etc.)(cont'd)

Ref	Name	Data	Average Condition Price Range £	$
R334	'V.P.K.' (type A non-Autog.)	pcc	15-30	25-50
> R335	'V.P.K.' (type B)	pcc	8-15	13-25
R336	'V.P.K.' (Tessar/Compur)	*	a. 150	a. 260
R337	'Vigilant Six-20' folding	**	14-17	25-30
S27	Rollfilm backs	*	a. 20	a. 35
KODAK also see FOLMER				
KODAK also see ROCHESTER OPTICAL				
KODAK A.G. (Stuttgart)				
> Q145	'Retina or Retina 1'	***	25-30	45-55
Q146	'Retina 1a or 1b'	**	40-50	70-85
Q147	'Retina 11 or 11a'	**	25-30	45-55
Q148	'Retina 11c'	pcc	30-60	55-110
Q149	'Retina 11S' c.r.f.	pcc	30-60	55-110
Q150	'Retina 111c' (NB sm c)	**	65-80	110-130
Q151	'Retina Reflex'	****	75-90	130-160
Q152	'Retinette' (various)	pcc	15-30	25-50
> R338	'Duo 620' (16 on 620)	pcc	15-30	25-50
R339	'Regent 1' c.r.f.	***	65-80	110-130
R340	'Suprema' (12 on 620)	*	a. 260	a. 460
R341	'Vollenda' (not NAGEL)	pcc	15-30	25-50
KODAK A.G. also see NAGEL/KODAK				
KOOPMAN (New York)				
S28	'Presto' sub-miniature (1896)	***	340-420	600-750
KONISHIROKU (Japan)				
Q153	'Autorex' S.L.R.	*	a. 55	a. 95
Q154	'Konica' c.r.f.	**	30-35	50-60
R342	'Konica Aerial G'	***	120-150	220-260
KORSTEN (Paris)				
P248	'Litote' stereo 45 * 107mm	*	a. 45	a. 80
KOWA (Japan)				
R343	'Auto-S' c.r.f. (126 film)	pcc	15-30	25-50
R344	'Kowaflex' S.L.R.	*	a. 170	a. 300
KRAUSS E. (Paris)				
P249	'Photo-Revolver'	**	340-420	600-750
P250	'Takyr' folding plate	**	85-100	140-170
Q155	'Eka' (100 exposures)	**	500-600	850-1000

> R335 'V.P.K. Model B'
... Introduced 1925 as a replacement for the Type A and made in G.B. from 1931. The same basic design but with a removable back was used for the Series 111 and V.P.K. Special and for variants in colour etc. such as the Boy Scout & Vanity Kodaks until c.1934.

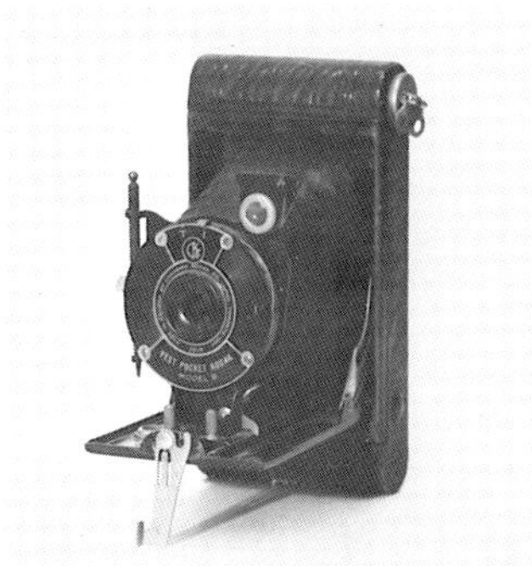

> Q145. 'Retina & Retina 1'
... This category covers all variants of the Retina and Retina 1 both pre- and post- war models. Usually with Xenar or Ektar f3.5 lens in Compur shutters there is little significant difference in value other than a small premium for the original 1934 version.

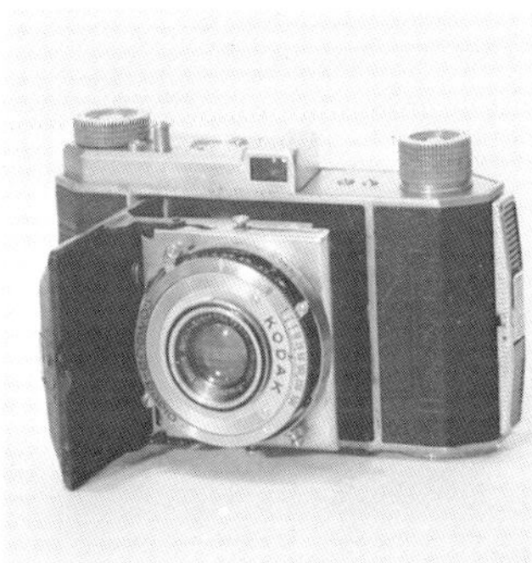

> R338. 'Duo 620'
... A horizontally styled folding camera for 16 exposures 4.5 * 6 cm. on 620 film. Kodak f 3.5 or f4.5 Anastigmat or f 3.5 Tessar lens in Compur or Compur-Rapid shutter. Series 1 cameras 1934 to 1937 and Series 11 1937 to 1939. R338 excludes the c.r.f. version.

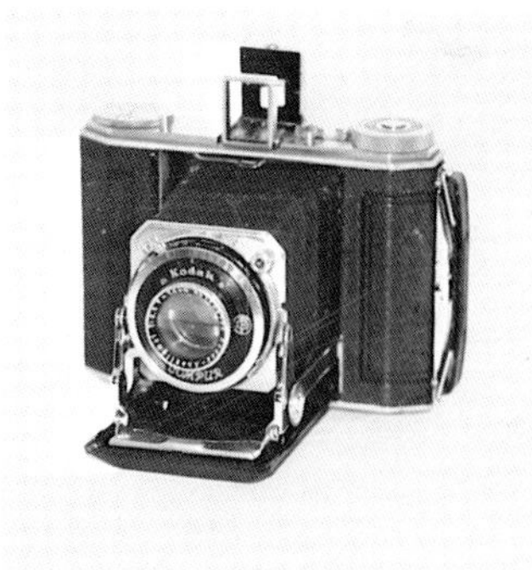

Ref	Name	Data	Average Condition Price Range £	$
KRAUSS G.A (Stuttgart)				
Q156	'Peggy 1' folding strut	**	240-300	420-500
R345	'Rollette' 5 * 7.5 cm	**	75-90	130-160
KRUGENER (Frankfurt)				
P251	Folding plate 9 * 12 cm.	**	25-30	45-55
P252	'Delta' detective	*	a. 100	a. 180
P253	'Patent Book Camera'	*	a. 1500	a. 2600
P254	'Periscop' H & S 9 * 12 cm.	*	a. 55	a. 95
P255	Stereo Hand & Stand 9 * 12 cm	*	a. 190	a. 340
R346	'Delta' rollfilm	**	70-85	120-150
KUNIK (Frankfurt)				
> S29	'Petitux' etc. 14 * 14 mm.	**	18-20	30-35
S30	'Petie Vanity'(ladies compact)	**	220-260	380-460
K.W. (Dresden)				
> P256	'Patent Etui'6.5 * 9 cm.	***	45-55	80-100
P257	'Patent Etui'6.5 * 9 cm outfit	*	a. 110	a. 190
P258	'Patent Etui'9 * 12 cm	**	60-75	110-130
Q157	'Praktiflex' S.L.R.	pcc	20-40	35-70
R347	'Pilot' S.L.R.	**	35-45	65-80
R348	'Pilot' folding T.L.R.	***	150-180	260-320
R349	'Reflex-Box' S.L.R.	**	40-50	70-85
K.W./PENTACON (Dresden)				
Q158	'Praktica' S.L.R.	**	25-30	45-55
Q159	'Prakticamat' S.L.R.	pcc	15-30	25-50
Q160	'Praktina FX' (Tessar 2.8)	pcc	30-60	55-110
R350	'Praktisix' S.L.R.	**	90-110	160-200
LANCASTER (Birmingham)				
P259	'Amateur Patent' field 1/2 pl	**	80-100	140-170
P260	Folding stereo 1/2 plate	*	a. 280	a. 500
P261	'Gem' (6 lens stamp)	*	a. 1700	a. 3000
> P262	'Instantograph' 1/4 plate	*****	95-100	160-180
P263	'Instantograph' 1/4 pl outfit	**	150-180	260-320
P264	'Instantograph' 1/2 plate	*****	85-95	150-170
P265	'International' tailboard	***	85-100	140-170
P266	'Kamret' field 1/2 plate	*	a. 50	a. 90
P267	'Kamrex' Hand & Stand 1/4 pl	*	a. 55	a. 95

> S29. 'Petitux' etc.
... One of a range of 16mm rollfilm (14 * 14 mm exposures) sub-miniature cameras with similar names starting Peti.. . Made in several versions some of which (e.g. the Walt Disney the flash synchronised and the gold plated) command premium prices. c.1950-60

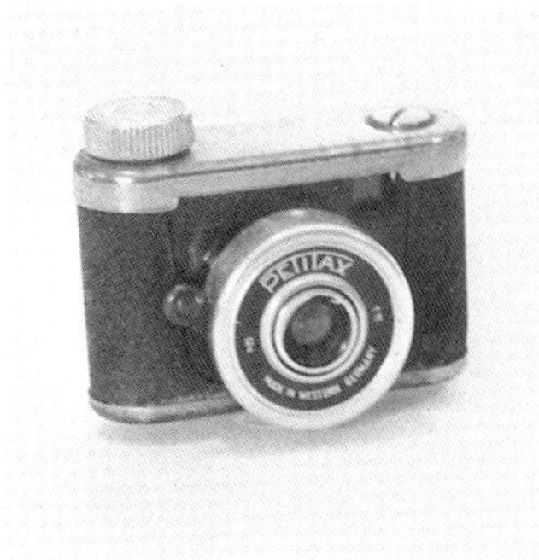

> P256. 'Patent Etui'
... A slim line folding plate camera on which the baseboard was slightly dished enabling the bellows lens and shutter to fit snugly inside the body when the camera was closed giving a highly pocketable shape. See also Ref. P258 for the 9 * 12 cm. size. c.192.-1939.

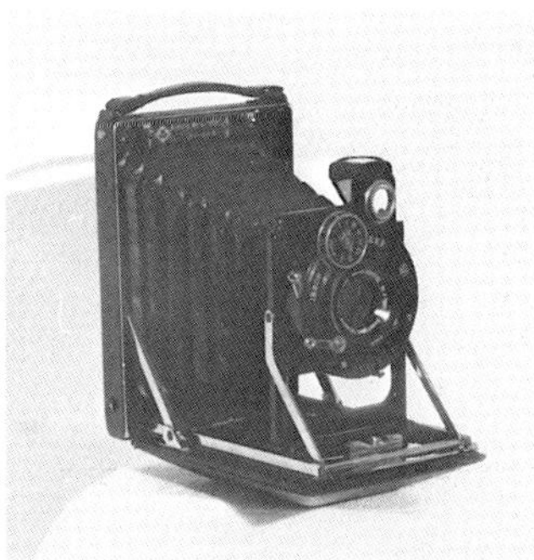

> P262. 'Instantograph'
... The generic name for a range of brass and mahogany view cameras by LANCASTER introduced c.1882. The type was distinguished by the design of the ground glass screen which was mounted with four special hinges. 'Instantographs' mostly had Lancaster lenses.

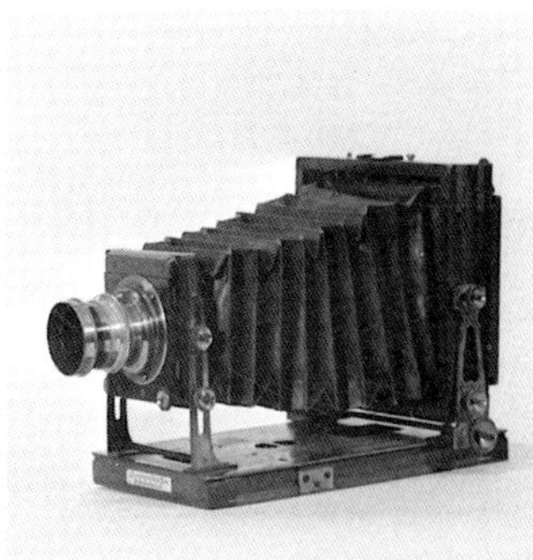

LANCASTER (Birmingham)(cont'd)

Ref	Name	Data	Average Condition Price Range £	$
P268	'Ladies' 1/4 plate	*	a. 700	a. 1200
P269	'Le Meritoire' folding 1/4 pl.	*	a. 85	a. 150
P270	'Le Merveilleux'	****	75-90	130-160
P271	Multiple exposure (4 lens)	**	1400-1700	2400-2900
P272	'Omnigraph' falling plate	**	30-35	50-60
P273	'Rover' detective falling pl	**	220-260	380-460
P274	'Special field' 1/4 plate	*	a. 160	a. 280
P275	Stereo field 7 * 3 1/2 in	*	a. 260	a. 460
> P276	'Stopit' falling plate	*	a. 90	a. 160
LAWLEY W (London)				
P277	Tailboard 6 * 6 in.	*	a. 80	a. 140
LE COULTRE (Switzerland)				
> S31	'Compass' min. 35mm roll film	****	550-650	1000-1200
LEECH & SCHMIDT (Germany)				
P278	Tailboard 13 * 18 cm	**	100-120	170-200
LEHMANN (Berlin)				
S32	'Ben Akiba' ? (canehandle)	*	a. 3000	a. 5300
LEIBE (Paris) see JEANNERET				
LEIDOLF (Wetzlar)				
Q161	'Lordomat' c.r.f.	*	a. 35	a. 60
LEITZ (Wetzlar) see page 68 for lenses & page 72 for ancillaries.				
T1	Replica 'UR-Leica'	**	800-1000	1400-1700
T2	'Leica 1'(Anast. 50mm f3.5)	*	a. 10500	a. 18500
T3	'Leica 1'mod-A (Elmax f3.5)	**	2400-2900	4200-5100
> T4	'Leica 1'mod-A 4-digit(Elmar)	***	420-500	700-850
T5	'Leica 1'mod-A 5-digit(Elmar)	*****	200-220	340-380
T6	'Leica 1' (Hektor f2.5)	*	a. 260	a. 460
T7	'Leica 1'mod-B(rim. Compur)	***	2000-2400	3400-4200
T8	'Leica 1'mod-B(dial. Compur)	**	2600-3200	4600-5600
T9	'Leica 1' model-C body	*	a. 75	a. 130
T10	'Leica 1' model-C	****	200-240	340-420
T11	'Leica 1'mod.C non-standard	*	a. 1700	a. 3000
T12	'Leica 1 Luxus' ?	*	a. 4400	a. 7700
T13	'Leica 11' body	**	60-75	110-130
T14	'Leica 11' (Elmar or Hektor)	*****	150-170	260-280
T15	'Leica 11'(Meyer Kinoplasmat)	*	a. 360	a. 650

> P276. 'Stopit'
...   A simple design of falling plate camera for 6 1/4 plates. Had a Lancaster patent rotary shutter; brass fittings and the unusual feature of a single viewfinder placed centrally above the lens. c.1900

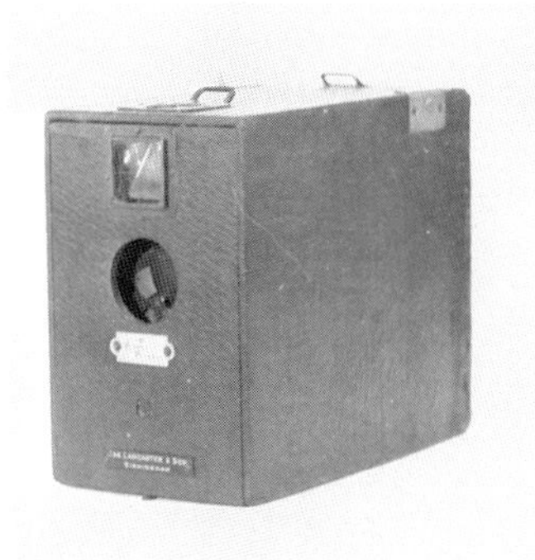

> S31. 'Compass'
...   c.1938. Placed in the miscellaneous group as it is both a 35mm and a plate camera. Probably one of the most complicated precision cameras made with a multitude of built-in facilities. It catered for almost any photographic use; usually successfully.

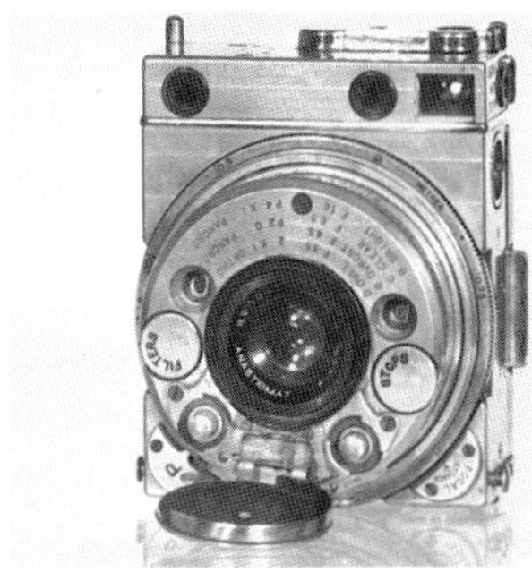

> T4. 'Leica 1' model A
...   This Leica had a black paint finish to the top and bottom plates; black body and non-interchangeable 50mm f3.5 Elmar lens. It was introduced 1926.The earlier 4-digit serial No models fetch higher prices than later ones (Ref. T5) which were produced until 1930.

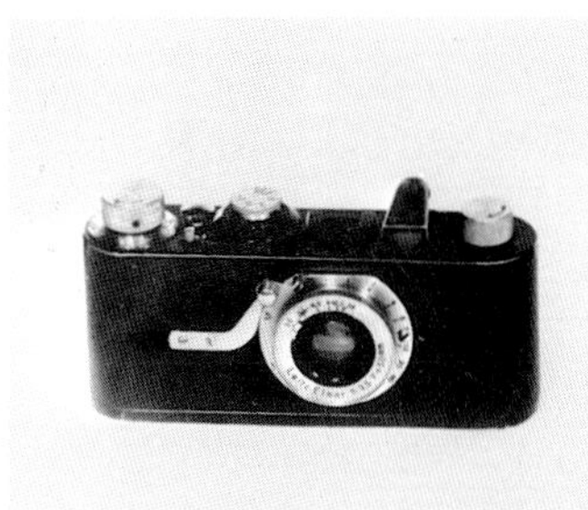

Ref	Name	Data	Average Condition Price Range £	$
T16	'Leica 11'(Summar/Summitar)	****	110-130	190-240
T17	'Leica Standard' body	**	70-85	120-150
T18	'Leica Standard'	****	150-180	260-320
T19	'Leica 111' body	**	65-80	110-130
T20	'Leica 111'(Leitz Eigentum)	*	a. 550	a. 950
T21	'Leica 111'(Elmar or Summar)	*****	110-120	190-200
T22	'Leica 111'(other lenses)	***	120-150	220-260
T23	'Leica Reporter 250..'	***	3700-4500	6400-7800
T24	'Leica Reporter K250'	*	a. 6600	a. 11500
T25	'Leica 111A' chrome body	***	75-90	130-160
T26	'Leica 111A'	*****	110-120	190-200
T27	'Leica 111A' display model	*	a. 420	a. 750
T28	'Leica 111A' monte en Sarre	*	a. 1200	a. 2100
T29	'Leica Single-shot'	**	260-320	460-550
T30	'Leica 111B' body	***	90-110	160-200
> T31	'Leica 111B'	****	130-150	220-260
T32	'Leica 111B' (Engaved base)	*	a. 650	a. 1100
T33	'Leica 111B' (Luft. Elmar)	*	a. 700	a. 1200
T34	'Leica 111C' body	**	70-85	120-150
T35	'Leica 111C' (military body)	**	850-1000	1400-1700
T36	'Leica 111C' grey Luft(Elmar)	**	850-1000	1400-1700
> T37	'Leica 111C' (Elmar)	****	120-140	200-240
T38	'Leica 111C'(Summitar/Summar)	*****	170-200	300-340
T39	'Leica 111C' (shark-skin)	*	a. 300	a. 550
T40	'Leica 111C' (Summarit f1.5)	*	a. 460	a. 800
T41	'Leica 11C'	***	130-160	220-260
T42	'Leica 1C'	***	180-220	320-400
T43	'Leica 111 D-type' body	*	a. 260	a. 460
T44	'Leica 111F' body	***	120-150	220-260
> T45	'Leica 111F' (Black Dial)	****	220-260	380-460
T46	'Leica 111F' (Red Dial)	****	140-170	240-300
T47	'Leica 111F'RD (Summicron f2)	**	220-260	380-460
T48	'Leica 111F'RD (d.a. timer)	***	180-220	320-400
T49	'Leica 11F'	**	160-200	280-340
T50	'Leica 1F'BD body	**	360-440	650-800
T51	'Leica 1F'BD (body AP8886)	*	a. 850	a. 1500

> T31. 'Leica 111B'
... Similar to the 111A but with minor improvements particularly the closer positioning of the range and viewfinder eyepieces. The 111B was last Leica with the 5 1/4 in. body length. Main production 1938 to 1940 with small quantities in 1941 and 1946.

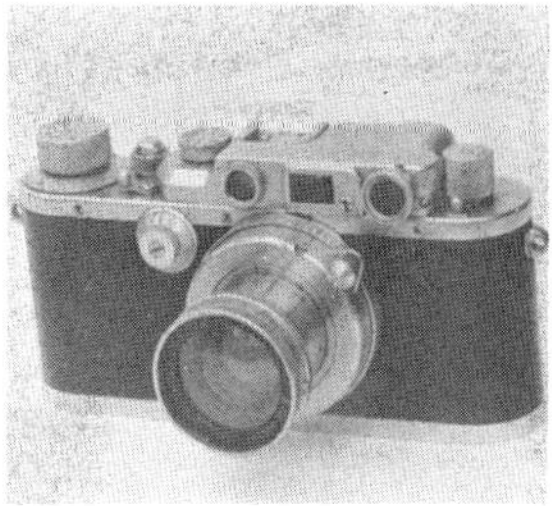

> T37. 'Leica 111C'
... The first Leica to have a diecast body and a one piece body and rangefinder cover. It was 1/8 in.longer than the 111B above.
In production from 1940 to 1951 and serial numbered in the range 360175 - 525000.

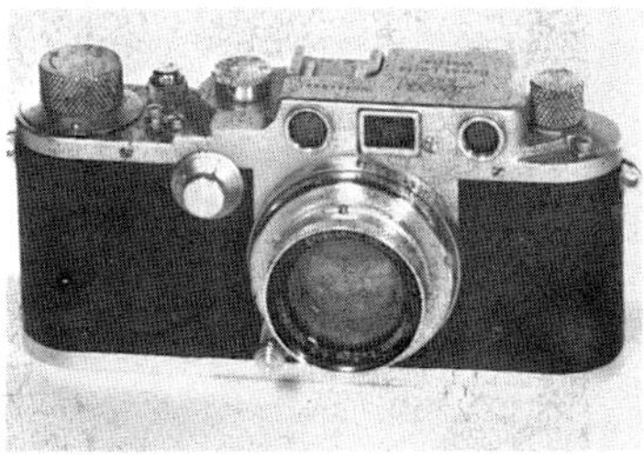

> T45. 'Leica 111F'
... T45 to T48 cover the three main types of the 111F The 'black dial' (refers to flash sync. Nos) 1950 to 1952 in serial No sequence 525001-611000; the 'red dial' 1952 to 1954 serial Nos to 685000 and the red dial with d.a. timer 1954 to 1957 serial Nos to 825000.

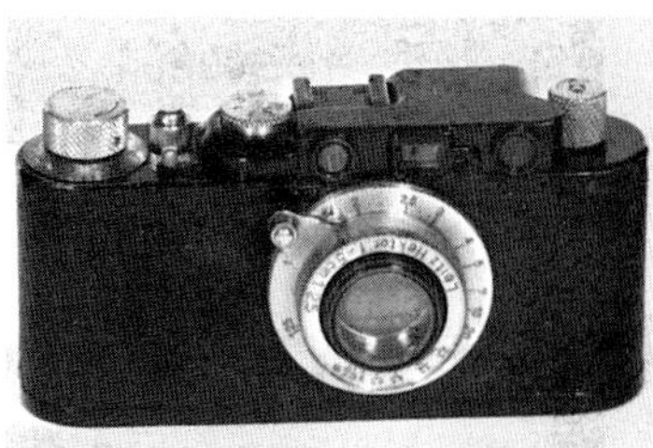

Ref	Name	Data	Average Condition Price Range £	$
T52	'Leica 1F'BD (Elmar f3.5)	***	380-460	650-800
T53	'Leica 1F'RD body	***	240-300	420-500
T54	'Leica 1F'RD (Elmar f3.5)	**	220-260	380-460
T55	'Leica 111G' dummy	*	a. 240	a. 420
T56	'Leica 111G' body	**	280-340	480-600
T57	'Leica 111G' (various lens)	*****	460-500	800-900
T58	'Leica 111G'(Super-Angulon f4)	*	a. 900	a. 1600
T59	'Leica 1G' body	**	460-550	800-1000
T60	'Leica M3' (demo model)	*	a. 3100	a. 5400
T61	'Leica M3' (Tiranty pres'tn)	*	a. 1800	a. 3200
T62	'Leica M3' dble stroke body	**	340-420	600-750
T63	'Leica M3' ds.olive green	*	a. 1100	a. 1900
T64	'Leica M3' ds. with lens	****	280-340	480-600
> T65	'Leica M3' single stroke	**	280-340	480-600
T66	'Leica M3' ss.olive green	*	a. 1100	a. 1900
T67	'Leica M3' ss. with lens	***	340-420	600-750
T68	'Leica M3' Betriebsk	*	a. 1300	a. 2300
T69	'Leica MP' body	**	4100-5000	7200-8800
T70	'Leica M2' dummy	*	a. 0	a. 0
T71	'Leica M2' cut-away demo.	*	a. 1100	a. 1900
T72	'Leica M2' body	***	280-340	480-600
T73	'Leica M2' military body	*	a. 4600	a. 8100
T74	'Leica M2' body with motor	**	1300-1600	2300-2800
T75	'Leica M2' (button rewind)	*	a. 700	a. 1200
> T76	'Leica M2' (+lens & access)	***	360-440	650-800
T77	'Leica M2' (gold plated)	*	a. 2400	a. 4200
T78	'Leica M2-R' (Summicron f2)	*	a. 1400	a. 2500
T79	'Leica M1' body	**	140-170	240-300
T80	'Leica M1' olive green body	*	a. 1300	a. 2300
T81	'Leica M1' (lever rewind)	*	a. 950	a. 1700
T82	'Leica MD' body	*	a. 280	a. 500
T83	'Leica MDPost'(Summaron f2.8)	***	650-800	1100-1300
T84	'Leica MDa'(army model Y)	*	a. 900	a. 1600
T85	'Leica M4'(dummy camera)	**	260-320	460-550
> T86	'Leica M4' body	***	650-800	1100-1300
T87	'Leica M4' 50 Anniv'sry body	*	a. 900	a. 1600

> T65 'Leica M3'
... The first Leica to use a bayonet lens mount it also had a common eyepiece for the view and range finders and bright line frames for 50 90 & 135 mm. lenses.
Introduced 1954 at serial No 700000. Last serial No was 1158995 in 1966.

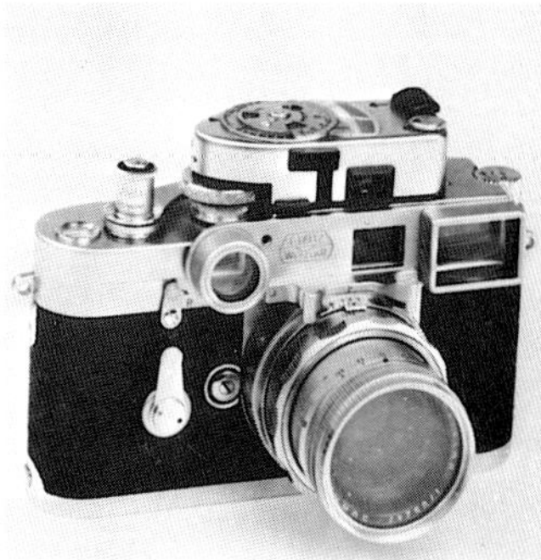

> T76. 'Leica M2'
... Introduced 1958 as as a wide-angle alternative to the 'tele' Leica at serial No 926000.
The 'M2' had an external manual reset film counter and viewfinder for 35 50 and 90 mm. lenses. Production ceased 1967 at serial No 1165000.

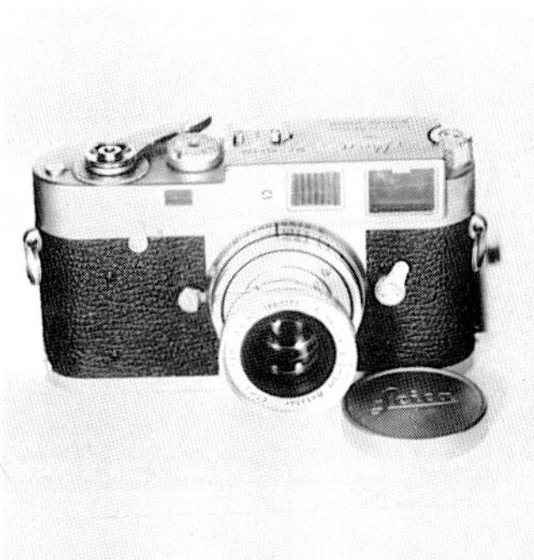

> T86. 'Leica M4'
... The 'M4' closely resembled the 'M2' but had a slanted rewind lever and an attached fold-away winder lever. There were also a number of minor finish differences.
In production 1967 to 1975. Serial Nos 1175001-1443170.

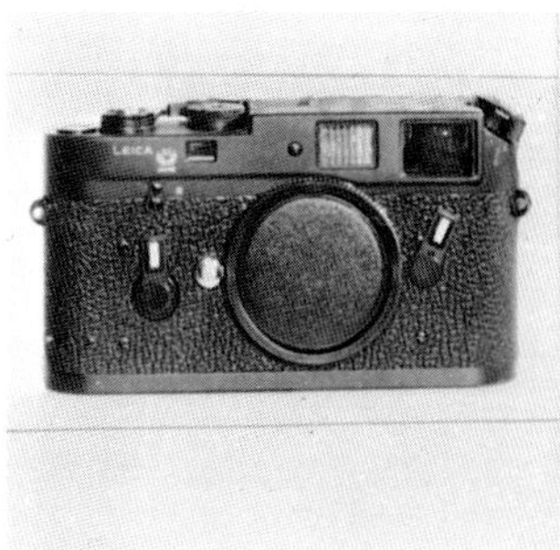

Ref	Name	Data	Average Condition Price Range £	$
T88	'Leica M4'(Summicron f2)	**	500-600	850-1000
T89	'Leica M4-MOT'& Leicamotor	*	a. 3200	a. 5600
T90	'Leica M4-M' body	*	a. 3700	a. 6500
T91	'Leica M4-P' (boxed)	*	a. 550	a. 950
T92	'Leica MDA' motorised body	*	a. 700	a. 1200
T93	'Leica M5' cut-away demo.	*	a. 1000	a. 1800
T94	'Leica M5'chr.in makers box	*	a. 750	a. 1300
T95	'Leica M5'(Summilux f1.4)	**	550-650	950-1200
> T96	'Leica CL' (Summicron-C)	**	280-340	480-600
T97	'Leica CL' outfit	*	a. 600	a. 1100
T98	'Leica M4-2' body	*	a. 360	a. 650
T99	'Leica M4-2'gold(Summilux)	*	a. 1000	a. 1800
T100	'Leica MD-2' body	*	a. 320	a. 550
T101	'Leicaflex SL' dummy	**	170-200	280-340
T102	'Leicaflex SL' body	**	120-150	220-260
T103	'Leicaflex or Leicaflex SL'	****	240-280	400-480
> T104	'Leicaflex SL'(Anniversary)	*	a. 600	a. 1100
T105	'Leicaflex SL MOT'(Summicron)	*	a. 480	a. 850
> T106	'Leica R3' black body	*	a. 150	a. 260
T107	'Leica R3' display body	*	a. 70	a. 120
T108	'Leica R3' silver chrome body	**	650-800	1100-1300
T109	'Leica R3 MOT'	**	240-300	420-500
T110	'Leica R3'green safari outfit	**	650-800	1100-1300
T111	'Leica R3' de-luxe Centenary	**	1300-1600	2300-2800
T112	'Leica R4S'(Summicron-R f2)	*	a. 300	a. 550
T113	'Elcan f2.8'	*	a. 40	a. 70
T114	'Elmar f3.5'	****	70-85	120-140
T115	'Elmar 50mm' Luftwaffen	*	a. 400	a. 700
T116	'Elmar 90mm f4' (rigid)	*****	65-70	110-120
T117	'Elmar 90mm f4' (fat-barrel)	***	220-260	380-460
T118	'Elmar 90mm f4' (collapsible)	***	140-170	240-300
T119	'Elmar 105mm f6.3'(mountain)	****	300-360	500-600
T120	'Elmar 135mm'telephoto(bay'nt)	**	75-90	130-160
T121	'Elmar 135mm'telephoto(screw)	*	a. 170	a. 300
T122	'Elmar 135mm f4.5'	***	60-75	110-130
T123	'Elmar-C 90mm f4'	*	a. 170	a. 300

> T96. 'Leica CL'
... Designed by LEITZ and made by MINOLTA in Japan the CL is a compact c.r.f. camera with a built-in through-the-lens metering system and focal plane shutter (1/2 to 1/1100 sec) operating vertically. A total of 65000 cameras were made between 1973 and 1976.

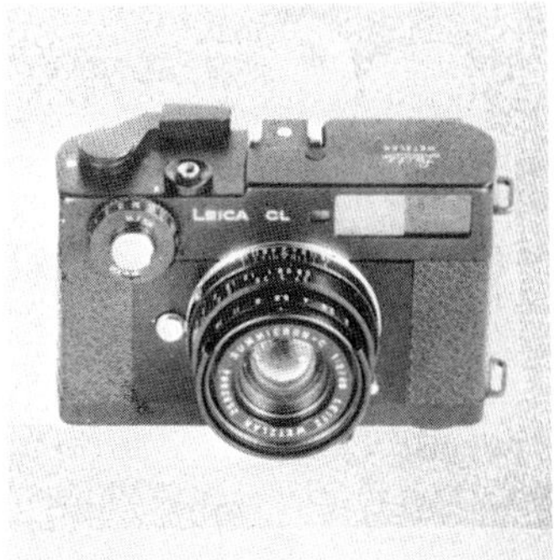

> T103. 'Leicaflex'
... The 'Leicaflex' was the first S.L.R. by LEITZ. Made from 1964 to 1968 (serial Nos 1080001 - 1174700) it was followed by the 'Leicaflex SL' in the period 1968 to 1974 (serial Nos 1173001-137500) and the 'SL2' from 1974 to 76 (serial Nos 1385001-144300).

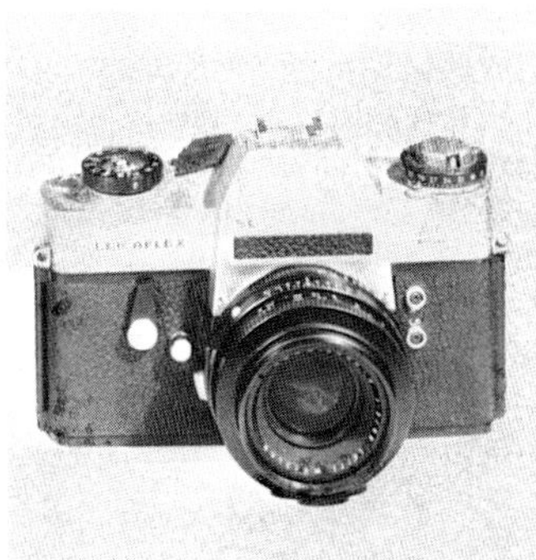

> T106. 'Leica R3'
... In 1976 Leitz introduced a new range of S.L.R. cameras with an electronic shutter variable from 4 sec. to 1/1000 sec; highly accurate metering system and a memory lock. The R3 was made in Wetzlar and in Portugal until 1979.

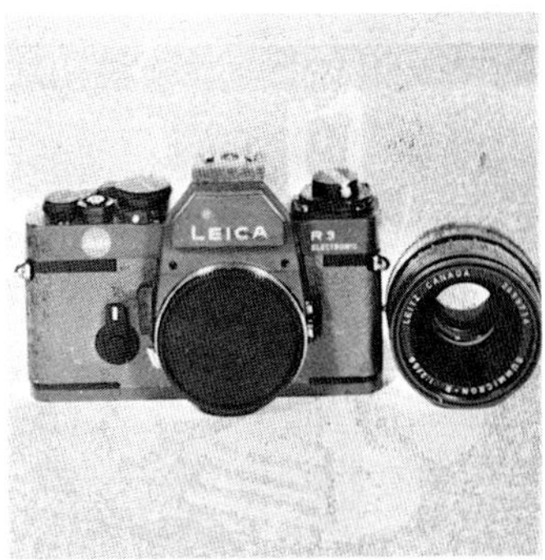

Ref	Name	Data	Average Condition Price Range £	$
T124	'Elmarit 28mm f2.8'	**	180-220	320-400
T125	'Elmarit 90mm f2.8'(bayonet)	**	110-130	190-240
T126	'Elmarit 90mm f2.8'(screw)	*	a. 360	a. 650
T127	'Elmarit 135 or 180mm f2.8'	**	180-220	320-400
T128	'Hektor 28mm f6.3'	***	140-170	240-300
T129	'Hektor 50mm f2.5'	***	130-160	220-260
T130	'Hektor 50mm f2.5' (AB)	*	a. 240	a. 420
T131	'Hektor 73mm f1.9'	***	180-220	320-400
T132	'Hektor 125mm f2.5' Wetzlar	*	a. 480	a. 850
T133	'Hektor 135mm f4.5'	****	75-85	130-150
T134	'Hektor 135mm f4.5' Luft.	**	280-340	480-600
T135	'Macro-Elmar 100mm f4'	*	a. 75	a. 130
T136	'Noctilux 50mm f2'	*	a. 420	a. 750
T137	'Stemar Stereo 33mm f3.5'	**	1800-2200	3200-3900
T138	'Summar 24mm rotary stereo'	*	a. 1000	a. 1800
T139	'Summar 50mm f2' (rigid)	**	550-650	950-1200
T140	'Summarex 85mm f1.5' & v/f	*	a. 500	a. 900
T141	'Summar 24mm Rotary Stereo'	*	a. 1000	a. 1800
T142	'Summaron 28mm f5.6'	***	140-170	240-300
T143	'Summaron 35mm f3.5'	****	75-90	130-160
T144	'Summaron 35mm f2.8'	***	140-170	240-300
T145	'Summarit 50mm f1.5'cut-away	*	a. 140	a. 240
T146	'Summarit 50mm f1.5'	***	70-85	120-150
T147	'Summicron 35mm f2'(bayonet)	*	a. 360	a. 650
T148	'Summicron 35mm f2'(screw)	*	a. 140	a. 240
T149	'Summicron-C 40mm f2'	*	a. 65	a. 110
T150	'Summicron 50mm f2'	**	130-160	220-260
T151	'Summicron-R 50mm f2 Mark 1'	*	a. 480	a. 850
T152	'Summicron 90mm f2'	**	240-300	420-500
T153	'Summicron 90mm f2' (SOOZI)	*	a. 420	a. 750
T154	'Summilux 35mm f1.4'	*	a. 160	a. 280
T155	'Summitar 50mm f2'	***	120-150	220-260
T156	'Super-Angulon 21mm' bayonet	**	200-240	340-420
T157	'Super-Angulon 21mm' screw	*	a. 650	a. 1100
T158	'Telyt 20cm f4 or 28cm'	***	180-220	320-400
T159	'Telyt 20cm f4.5'	*	a. 90	a. 160

Ref	Name	Data	Average Condition Price Range £	$
T160	'Telyt 400mm f5'	***	360-440	650-800
T161	'Telyt 400mm f5' 1st model	*	a. 700	a. 1200
T162	'Prototype 400mm f8'	*	a. 1100	a. 1900
T163	'Telyt 560mm'	**	380-460	650-800
T164	'Thambar 90mm f2.2'	***	600-750	1100-1300
T165	'Xenon 50mm f1.5'	**	130-160	220-260
T166	'Bellows set UXMOOR'	*	a. 40	a. 70
T167	'Copying set BOOWU'	***	30-35	50-60
T168	'Flash unit Chico'	*	a. 30	a. 55
T169	'Focaslide' OOGAN	*	a. 55	a. 95
T170	'Focomat' vertical enlarger	*	a. 85	a. 150
T171	'Focus attachment NOOKY'	*	a. 20	a. 35
T172	Handgrip for Leicaflex	*	a. 70	a. 120
T173	'Leicaflex' motor	***	160-200	280-340
T174	'Leicameters'	***	40-50	70-85
T175	'Leicavit' baseplate	*	a. 110	a. 190
T176	'Leica Motor'(2 speed)+MOOLY	**	700-850	1200-1500
T177	'Micro attachment MIKAS'	**	70-85	120-150
T178	'Micro camera MICCA'	*	a. 120	a. 220
T179	'Micro viewer MIKAM'	*	a. 120	a. 220
T180	'Motor drive arm MOOLY'	***	75-90	130-160
T181	'Plumb line FLOTH'	*	a. 180	a. 320
T182	'Rangefinders FOKOS & FODUA'	***	35-45	65-80
T183	'Rangefinder HFOOK'	*	a. 110	a. 190
T184	'Rapid winder SCNOO'	**	140-170	240-300
T185	'Remote shutter rlse OOFRC'	*	a. 850	a. 1500
T186	'Slow speed attachment HEBOO'	**	130-160	220-260
T187	'Stereoslide FIATE'	*	a. 110	a. 190
T188	'Stereoscope Viewer VOTRA'	**	200-240	340-420
T189	'Stereoly' beam splitter	**	650-800	1100-1300
T190	'Synchronizer CAVOO'	*	a. 35	a. 60
T191	Tripods table and heads	***	35-45	65-80
T192	'Triple Lens Turret OROLF'	*	a. 260	a. 460
T193	Underwater housing by A.U.K.	*	a. 700	a. 1200
T194	'Viewfinder AUFSOO'	***	65-80	110-130
T195	'Viewfinder SBOOI'	**	18-20	30-35

Ref	Name	Data	Average Condition Price Range £	$
T196	'Viewfinder VIDOM'	***	35-45	65-80
T197	'Viewfinder VIOOH'	***	40-50	70-85
T198	'Viewfinder AYOOC'	*	a. 170	a. 300
T199	'Viewfinder SOOUT'	*	a. 100	a. 180
T200	'Viewfinder VISET'	**	110-130	190-240
T201	'Viewfinder VISOR'	*	a. 110	a. 190
T202	'Viewfinder VIZMO'	*	a. 340	a. 600
T203	'Viewfinders Rt.angled' WINTU	***	40-50	70-85
T204	'Visoflex 1 or 11'	****	90-110	160-200
T205	'Visoflex 1' (with lens)	***	120-150	220-260
T206	'Visoflex 111' (Elmar f3.5)	*	a. 130	a. 220
LE ROY (Paris)				
P279	'Le Stereo Panoramique'6 * 13	***	100-120	170-200
LEULLIER (Paris)				
P280	'Summum Special'stereo 6 * 13	**	65-80	110-130
LEVY S.J (London)				
P281	'Minia' Hand & Stand 1/4 pl.	*	a. 35	a. 60
> P282	'Pullman' detective 5 * 7 in	*	a. 1800	a. 3200
LINHOF (Munich)				
P283	Technical camera (not outfits)	***	140-170	240-300
LIPPISCHE (Barntrup)				
R351	'Flexora' T.L.R.	pcc	10-20	18-35
R352	'Rollop' T.L.R.	**	18-20	30-35
LIZARS (Glasgow)				
> P284	'Challenge' H & S 1/4 plate	****	110-130	200-240
P285	'Challenge'H & S 1/4 pl trop	**	240-300	420-500
P286	'Challenge' field	**	70-85	120-150
P287	'Challenge' stereo H & S	**	380-460	650-800
> R353	'Challenge Dayspool'	**	45-55	80-100
R354	'Challenge' 2 1/4 * 2 1/4 in	**	140-170	240-300
R355	'Challenge' stereo	*	a. 300	a. 550
R356	'Challenge' stereo tropical	*	a. 400	a. 700
R357	'Challenge' tropical rollfilm	***	240-300	420-500
LLOYD F (Liverpool)				
P288	Detective boxform 1/4 pl	*	a. 60	a. 110

>P282. 'Pullman Detective' ... A detective camera c.1903 for 5 * 7 in. plates made by S.J.LEVY who were absorbed by HOUGHTON's c.1906. It resembled a small leather case whose base dropped down to reveal the lens and bellows. Loaded by lifting the lid of the case to insert the dark slides.

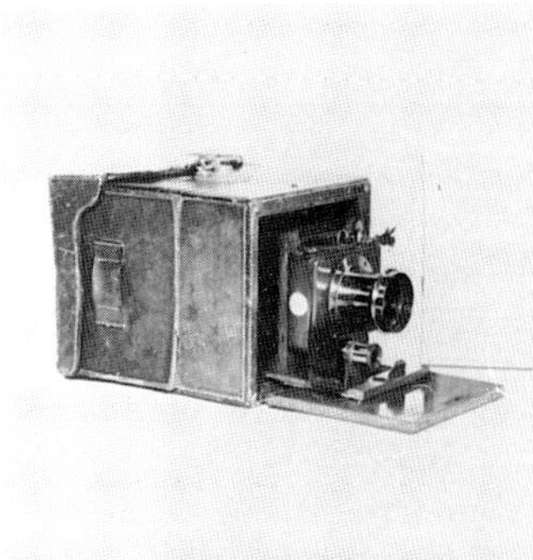

> P284. 'Challenge' H & S ... The 1/4 plate hand and stand was the most popular of LIZAR's cameras nearly all of which appear to have been called 'Challenge'. This model is very well designed and made to be a worthy rival (challenger?) to the better known 'Sanderson'. c.1905.

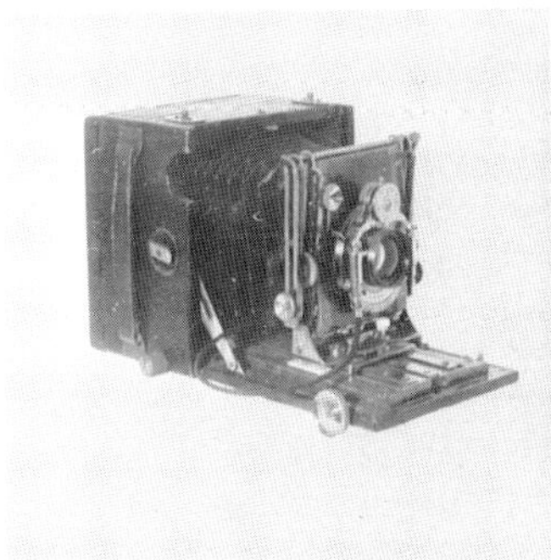

> R353. 'Challenge Dayspool' ... LIZAR's rollfilm range of cameras were all called 'Dayspool'. They were horizontally syled folding bed cameras for 1/4 or 1/2 plate with red or black bellows. The normal model was finished in leather and the tropical in polished mahogany. c.1905.

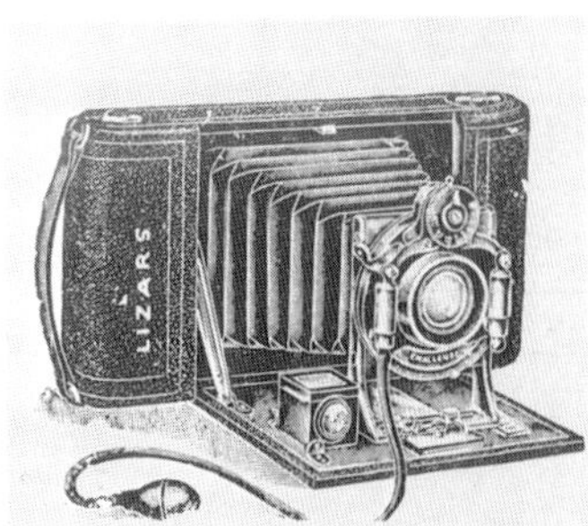

Challenge Dayspool - c1905. 3¼x4¼"

LOMO (Leningrad)

Ref	Name	Data	Average Condition Price Range £	$
R409	'Sputnik' stereo 6 * 13 cm	*	a. 90	a. 160
Q162	'Lomo 135 BC' (spring-wound)	pcc	5-10	9-18
LONDON STEREO. Co. (London)				
P289	'Artists Reflex' T.L.R.	**	180-220	320-400
> P290	'Binocular' (by Carpentier)	****	65-75	110-130
P291	'Carlton' T.L.R.	**	120-150	220-260
> P292	'Roylex' 6.5 * 9 cm.	*	a. 150	a. 260
P293	Sliding box wet plate 1/4 pl.	*	a. 600	a. 1100
P294	'Standard' 1/2 pl field	**	65-80	110-130
P295	Stereo changing box camera	*	a. 380	a. 650
P296	Tailboard 1/2 plate	**	110-130	190-240
P297	Tailboard wet/dry transitional	*	a. 200	a. 360
P298	Twin Lens Reflex 1/2 plate	*	a. 150	a. 260
P299	'Vesca' V.P. strut	**	180-220	320-400
R358	'Kings Own' tropical	**	850-1000	1400-1700
LUMIERE (Paris)				
R359	'Elax' 3 * 4 cm.	*	a. 260	a. 460
R360	'Stereolux' 6 * 13 cm.	*	a. 80	a. 140
> S33	'Eljy' sub-miniature	***	30-35	50-60
LYTAX (Freiburg)				
Q163	Gun bore record camera	*	a. 30	a. 55
MACKENSTEIN (Paris)				
P300	Boxform tropical 13 * 18 cm	*	a. 100	a. 180
P301	Stereo jumelle	**	100-120	170-200
P302	Stereo/mono folding 13 * 18 cm	**	40-50	70-85
MACRIS & BOUCHER (Paris)				
P303	'Nil Melior' stereo 6 * 13 cm	**	55-65	95-120
MAGIC INTRODUCTION (New York)				
S34	'Photoret' watch camera	***	280-340	480-600
MAGNACAM (New Jersey)				
S35	'Wristmatic' wrist camera	**	45-55	80-100
MAMIYA (Tokyo)				
P304	Mamiya press 2 1/2 * 3 1/2 in	**	25-30	45-55
Q164	'Prismat' S.L.R.	pcc	30-60	55-110
R361	'Mamiyaflex' T.L.R.	**	30-35	50-60
R362	'Super 23' press camera	*	a. 90	a. 160
S36	'Mamiya-16' or 'Konan-16'	**	14-17	25-30

> P290. 'Binocular'

... Made by J.CARPENTIER in Paris and sold by the L.S.Co in the U.K.
The name comes from its appearance.Several versions were made from V.P. size upwards; all had a built-in plate changer. Said to be the first camera for use at eye-level. c.1898.

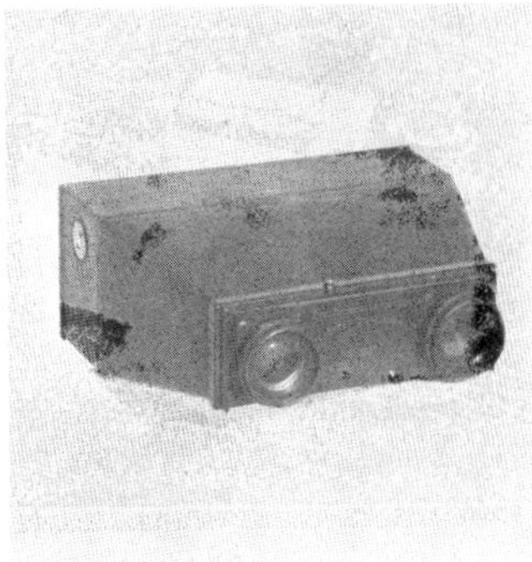

> P292. 'Roylex'

... This was actually a No 7 'Sibyl' made by NEWMAN & GUARDIA (see Ref. P342 page 84) to an L.S.Co. specification. It was the subject of threatened legal action by NEWMAN & GUARDIA when the L. S.Co. tried to get a copy made by another company.

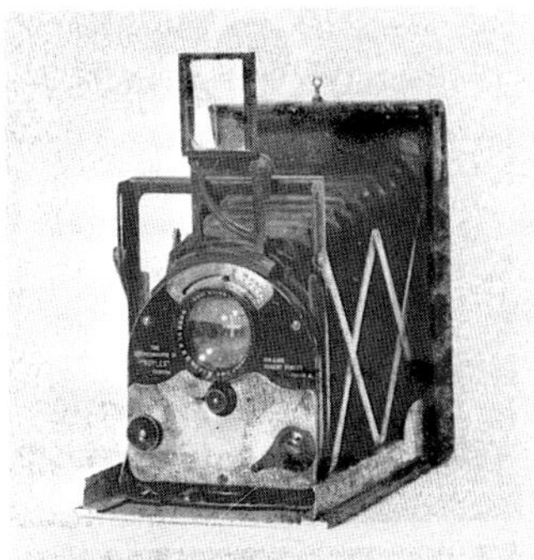

> S33. 'Eljy'

... A very small bodied camera taking 24 * 36 mm exposures on special rollfilm. The camera is dominated by the shutter which carries the f3.5 50mm Lypar lens.
Parallax correction can carried out on the viewfinder. 1937 to 1948.

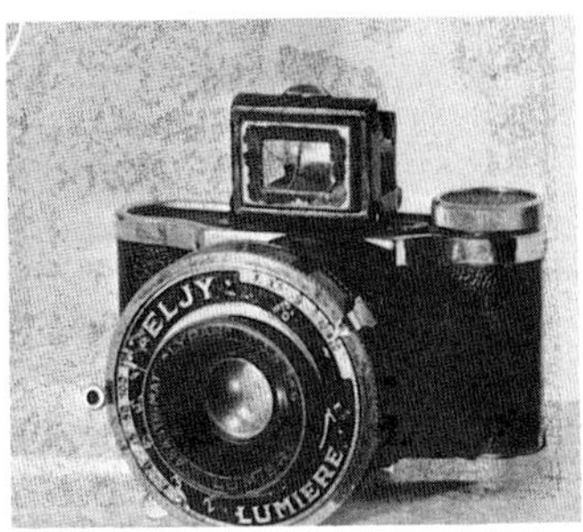

Ref	Name	Data	Average Condition Price Range £	$
MANHATTAN OPTICAL (New York)				
> P305	'Wizard' Hand and Stand	***	55-65	95-120
MARION/SOHO (London)				
P306	'All Metal Miniature'	***	1300-1600	2300-2800
P307	'Perfection' field 15 * 12	*	a. 180	a. 320
> P308	'Soho' reflex	****	70-85	120-150
P309	'Soho' reflex tropical	***	1100-1300	1900-2300
P310	'Soho' reflex V.P.	*	a. 550	a. 950
P311	'Soho Precision' H & S 6 * 9	*	a. 460	a. 800
P312	Sliding Box T.L.R	*	a. 1100	a. 1900
P313	Strut 6.5 * 9 cm.	*	a. 45	a. 80
P314	Tailboard 1/1 plate	**	120-150	220-260
MARLOW BROS (England)				
P315	'MB' field 1/4 & 1/2 pl	***	55-65	95-120
P316	'MB' field 1/1 plate	*	a. 120	a. 220
MARTIN H. (Paris)				
P317	Tailboard 17.5 * 13 cm	*	a. 60	a. 110
MASHPRIBORINTORG /KIEV (USSR)				
> Q165	'Kiev' (Contax copy)	**	18-20	30-35
S37	'Kiev 30' sub-miniature 16mm	**	30-40	55-75
S38	'Vega' sub-miniature 16mm	**	20-30	35-55
MASON (Glasgow)				
P318	Tailboard 12 * 10 in.	*	a. 70	a. 120
MAURER J (New York)				
R363	Aerial camera outfit (70mm)	*	a. 300	a. 550
McKELLEN (England)				
P319	'Treble Patent' field	**	80-100	140-170
MEAGHER (London)				
P320	Tailboard transitional 1/1pl	*	a. 190	a. 340
P321	Wet plate studio camera	**	280-340	480-600
MEOPTA (Prague)				
R364	'Flexarette' T.L.R.	pcc	8-15	13-25
S39	'Mikroma' sub-miniature 16mm	**	110-130	190-240
MERKEL (Germany)				
P322	'Phoenix'9 * 12 cm trop.fold.	**	120-150	220-260

> P305. 'Wizard'
... A range of American style hand and stand cameras in 5 * 4 and 5 * 7 in. sizes going under various names such as Junior or Senior or Baby or Cycle Wizard. A well made range of cameras similar in construction to others of the same origin and vintage. c.1895.

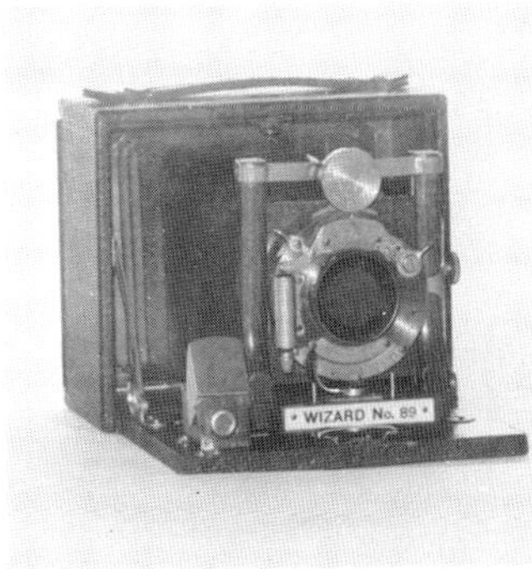

> P308. 'Soho Reflex'
... Probably the best known S.L.R. made in England between the world wars. This was due in part to the ingenious and elegant design of the mirror mechanism. It was made by KERSHAW's and sold under various names most notably by MARION's as the 'Soho'.

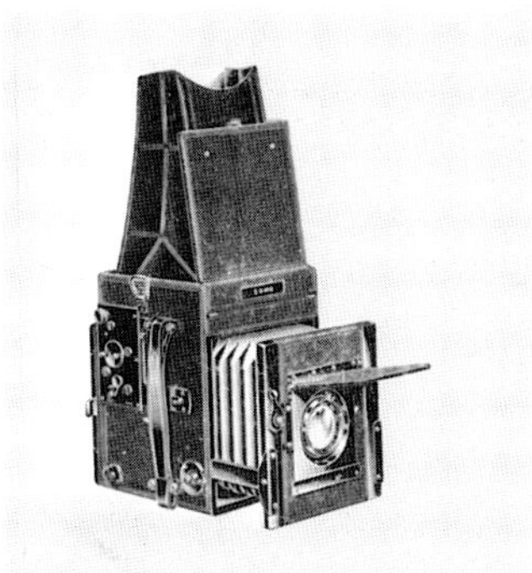

> Q165. 'Kiev'
... A series of coupled rangefinder cameras made in the USSR perhaps using the original 'Contax' tools. Best known are the 'Kiev 2' (= 'Contax 11') and 'Kiev 1V' (= 'Contax 111') which has a built-in exposure meter. The first USSR made Kiev's appeared in 1949.

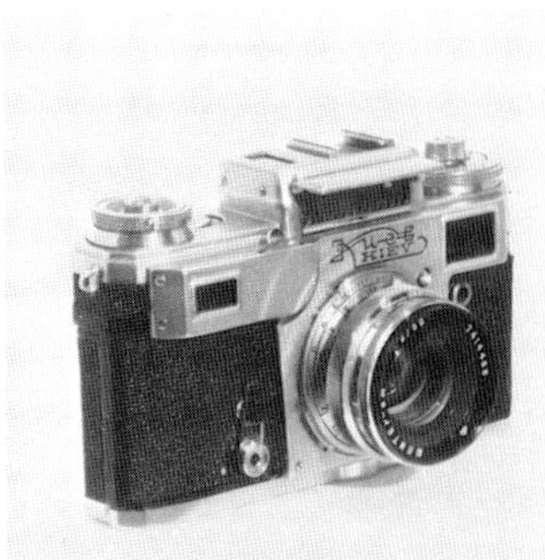

Ref	Name	Data	Average Condition Price Range £	$
MIKUT (Dresden)				
P323	'Mikut' 3-colour one-shot	*	a. 1300	a. 2300
MILBURN KORONA (Rochester)				
P324	Hand & Stand 1/2 plate	*	a. 80	a. 140
MINOLTA (Osaka)				
Q166	'Minolta SR1'	*	a. 20	a. 35
Q167	'Minolta SRM' (with motor)	*	a. 180	a. 320
Q168	'Minolta 35' (Leica copy)	**	70-85	120-150
R365	'Autocord' T.L.R.	**	45-55	80-100
S40	'Minolta 16P' sub-miniature	pcc	8-15	13-25
MINOX (Wetzlar & see VALSTS)				
S41	'Minox A' sub-miniature	**	60-75	110-130
S42	'Minox B' sub-min. (chrome)	***	45-55	80-100
S421	'Minox B' sub-min. (black)	**	90-120	160-220
S43	'Minox C' sub-miniature	****	70-85	120-150
MIRANDA (Tokyo)				
Q169	'Automex' S.L.R.	*	a. 55	a. 95
Q170	'Sensorex' S.L.R.	*	a. 30	a. 55
Q171	'Sensormat' S.L.R.	**	35-45	65-80
MOLLIER (Paris)				
Q172	'Le Cent Vues' (100 exp.)	**	380-460	650-800
MONROE (New York)				
P325	Hand & Stand cameras	**	35-45	65-80
MOORE (Liverpool)				
S44	'Aptus' ferrotype	***	30-35	50-60
S45	'Aptus' with tank & pick-up	**	80-100	140-170
MOORSE (London)				
P326	Studio camera with stand	*	a. 200	a. 360
MORITA (Japan)				
S46	'Kiku' novelty sub-min. 16mm	pcc	20-40	35-70
MORLEY W. (London)				
P327	'New Universal' tailboard	**	75-90	130-160
P328	Wet plate bellows camera	**	200-240	340-420
M.P.P. (Kingston-on-Thames)				
P329	'Micro Press' 5 * 4 in.	*	a. 110	a. 190
R366	'Microcord' T.L.R.	**	20-25	35-45
R367	'Microflex' T.L.R.	**	35-45	65-80

MULTISCOPE (Burlington)

Ref	Name	Data	Average Condition Price Range £	$
R368	'Al-Vista' panoramic	**	140-170	240-300
MURER (Milan)				
> P330	'Sprite' 4.5 * 6 cm.	**	40-50	70-85
P331	Stereo strut V.P.	*	a. 75	a. 130
MURRAY T.C (England)				
P332	Tailboard 1/1 plate	*	a. 110	a. 190
MUSASHINO KOKI (Japan)				
R369	'Rittreck 11a'S.L.R. 6 * 9cm	*	a. 220	a. 380
MUTSCHLER ROBINSON see RAY				
MYSTIC PLATE (New York)				
S47	'Mystic' button tintype	*	a. 45	a. 80
NAGEL/KODAK A.G. (Stuttgart)				
P333	Folding plate cameras	**	45-55	80-100
R370	'Pupille or Rolloroy'	**	110-130	190-240
R371	'Pupille or Rolloroy'(Elmar)	***	220-260	380-460
R372	'Ranca' (16 on 127)	*	a. 75	a. 130
> R373	'Vollenda' 3 * 4 cm.	**	50-60	85-100
R374	'Vollenda' (Elmar lens)	**	180-220	320-400
NATIONAL CAMERA (England)				
> P334	Field cameras	**	130-160	220-260
NAYLOR (London)				
P335	Field 1/1 plate	**	95-120	170-200
NEIDIG (Plankstadt)				
Q173	'Perlux' 24 * 24 mm	pcc	5-10	9-18
NEMROD (Japan)				
Q174	'Silura' underwater camera	**	30-35	50-60
NEGRETTI & ZAMBRA (London)				
P336	'Kinnears pat.' wet pl 7 * 6	*	a. 240	a. 420
NEOCO (Japan)				
Q175	'Neoca' (Leica copy)	pcc	15-30	25-50
NETTEL (Sontheim-Heilbronn)				
P337	'Deckrullo' strut 1/4 plate	*	a. 80	a. 140
P338	'Deckrullo' 6.5 * 9 cm tropica	*	a. 220	a. 380
NEW IDEAS (New York)				
Q176	'Tourist Multiple' outfit	*	a. 1100	a. 1900

> P330. 'Sprite'
... A popular V.P. vertical format strut plate camera made in Italy. Sold in England by City Sale and Exchange under their 'SALEX' trade name. Rapid-Aplanat f8 lens in simple two speed shutter. c. 1925.

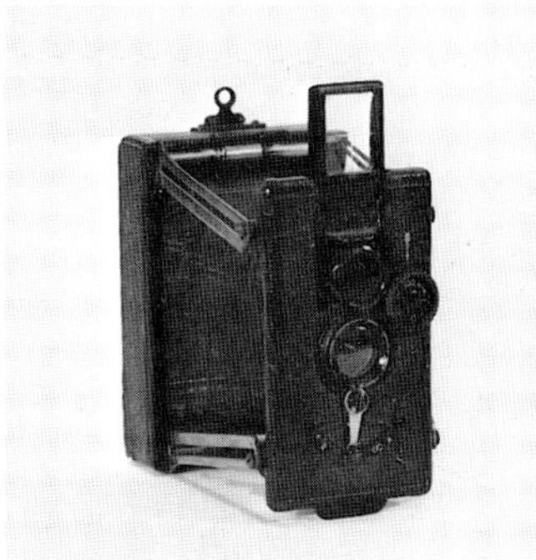

> R373. 'Vollenda'
... The 3 * 4 cm. Vollenda was made in Stuttgart by Dr NAGEL-WERK from 1931 and then by KODAK A.G. from the following year until 1937. This category covers all the lens and shutter variants except for the Elmar lens models which are part of Ref. R374.

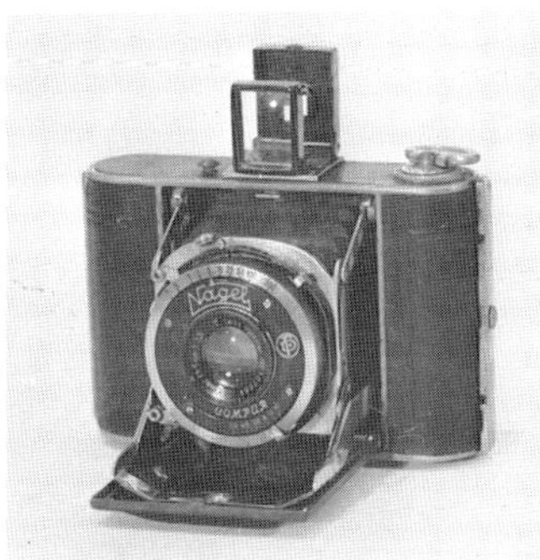

> P334. NATIONAL field
... A well constructed brass and mahogany field camera made 'for the trade'. It was deservedly popular and stocked by many independant dealers. c.1900. The 1/4 plate version is particularly attractive.

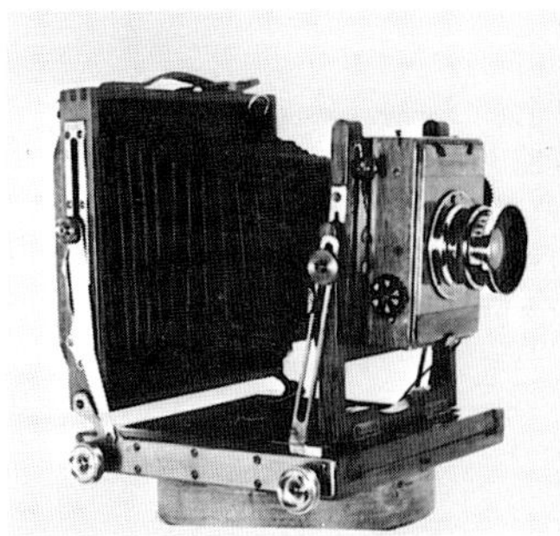

Ref	Name	Data	Average Condition Price Range £	$
> P339	Folding reflex 6.5 * 9 cm	****	120-140	200-240
P340	'Nydia'	***	260-320	460-550
P341	'Sibyl' 4.5 * 6 (Baby Sibyl)	****	200-240	360-440
> P342	'Sibyl' 6.5 * 9 cm	****	100-120	180-220
P343	'Sibyl' 1/4 plate	****	110-130	200-240
P344	'Sibyl Imperial' 1/4 plate	*	a. 160	a. 280
P345	'Sibyl' postcard	**	160-200	280-340
P346	'Special B' 1/4 plate	****	110-130	190-220
P347	'Universal' 1/4 plate	****	150-180	260-320
R375	Prototype 2 1/2 * 3 1/2 T.L.R.	*	a. 700	a. 1200
R376	'Sibyl' rollfilm V.P.	*	a. 150	a. 260
R377	'Sibyl' rollfilm (not V.P.)	***	150-180	260-320
NEWMAN & SINCLAIR (London)				
P348	Reflex 1/4 plate	*	a. 130	a. 220
NEWTON (Liverpool)				
P349	Tailboard	*	a. 90	a. 160
NICCA (Tokyo)				
Q177	'Nicca' (Leica 11 copy)	**	130-160	220-260
Q178	'Nicca type 3' body	*	a. 70	a. 120
NICHOLS (Liverpool)				
P350	Detective 1/4 plate	*	a. 45	a. 80
NIHON SHOKAI (Tokyo)				
R378	'Waltzflex' T.L.R.	pcc	10-20	18-35
NIKON (Tokyo)				
Q179	'Nikkorex Zoom' S.L.R.	***	45-55	80-100
Q180	'Nikon S' (Contax style)	***	140-170	240-300
Q181	'Nikon S' outfits	**	300-360	500-600
Q182	'Nikon SP' (motor driven)	**	280-340	480-600
NOAKES (London)				
P351	Field 1/1 plate	*	a. 70	a. 120
NORITA (Japan)				
R379	'Norita' 6 * 6 cm. S.L.R.	**	120-150	220-260
NORTON (New York)				
> R380	'Norton' (black plastic)	**	25-30	45-55
O.M.I (Rome)				
Q183	'Sunshine' tri-colour	**	140-170	240-300

> P339. Folding Reflex
... A very elegantly designed camera made only in 6.5 * 9 cm. size in two versions; the 'Standard' with a tilting lensboard and the 'Special' which took large aperture lenses. Both with a focal plane shutter and the characteristic very tall focussing hood.

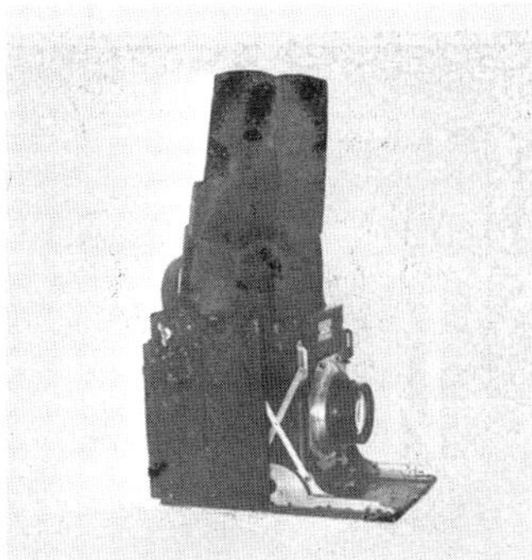

> P342. 'Sibyl'
... NEWMAN & GUARDIA's range of plate filmpack and rollfilm folding trellis cameras of such excellent design that they were made for over thirty years after their debut c. 1907.
Made in various sizes of which the V.P. and postcard are now the most scarce.

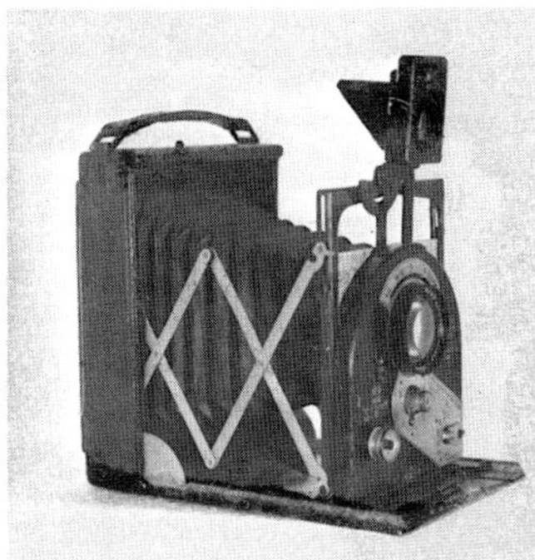

> R380. 'Norton'
... An inexpensive black plastic camera for 6 exposures 1 1/8 * 1 1/2 in. on special rollfilm and spool which also formed the winder. c. 1934.
The same design sold by the UNIVERSAL CAMERA Corp. of Chicago c. 1935 as the 'Norton-Univex'.

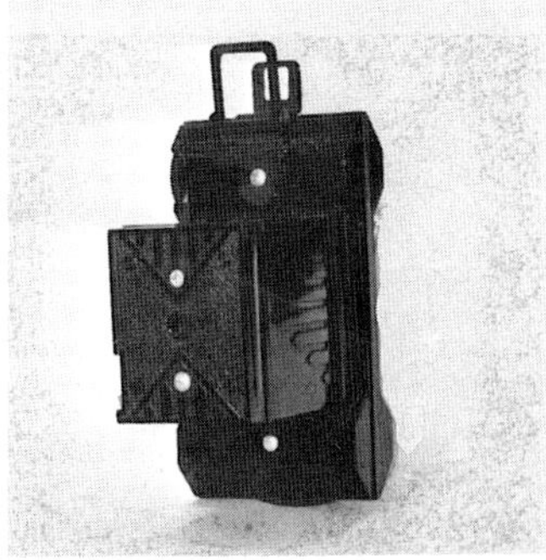

Ref	Name	Data	Average Condition Price Range £	$
OLBIA (Paris)				
R381	T.L.R. style box	pcc	8-15	13-25
OLYMPUS (Japan)				
Q184	'Auto-eye'	pcc	8-15	13-25
> Q185	'Pen S' or 'Pen EE'	***	25-30	45-55
Q186	'Pen F' or 'Pen FT'	***	75-90	130-160
R382	'Olympus 6 No 111A'	**	35-45	65-80
O.P.L (France)				
Q187	'Foca' (Leica copy)	**	40-50	70-85
ORION (Hanover)				
P352	'Rio' tropical 9 * 12 cm.	*	a. 220	a. 380
P353	'Rio' 6.5 * 9 cm (Tessar)	pcc	15-30	25-50
R383	'Daphne' folding V.P.	**	13-16	25-30
OSTERREICH TELEPHON (Vienna)				
> Q188	'Amourette' 24 * 30 mm	*	a. 160	a. 280
OTTEWILL (London)				
P354	Wet plate sliding box	*	a. 1800	a. 3200
PANON (Japan)				
Q189	'Widelux F7'(panoram) outfit	*	a. 950	a. 1700
PARK (London)				
P355	Field 1/2 plate	*	a. 90	a. 160
P356	Tailboard 1/1 plate	*	a. 35	a. 60
PEELING & VAN NECK (London)				
P357	Press camera fps	***	40-50	70-85
P358	Technical camera outfit	*	a. 150	a. 260
PENTACON see ZEISS/PENTACON				
PERKEN SON & RAYMENT (London)				
P359	Field 1/2 plate	**	95-120	170-200
P360	'Optimus' detective 1/4 pl	*	a. 120	a. 220
> P361	Tailboard 1/2 or 1/1 plate	****	90-110	160-200
P362	Tailboard 7 * 5 in or 1/4 pl.	**	120-150	220-260
PETSCHLER (Manchester)				
P363	Stereo wet/dry plate	*	a. 3600	a. 6300
PHOTOAVIT see BOLTA				
PHOTO DEVELOPMENTS (Birmingham)				
R384	'Envoy Wide-angle'	****	60-75	110-130

> Q185. 'Pen S and EE'
... These were 35mm half frame cameras for 18 * 24 mm. format.
The 'EE' was fitted with a Zuiko f3.5 28 mm. and the 'S' with Zuiko f2.8 30 mm. lens; both in synchronized six speed shutter and auto exposure control. c.1960.

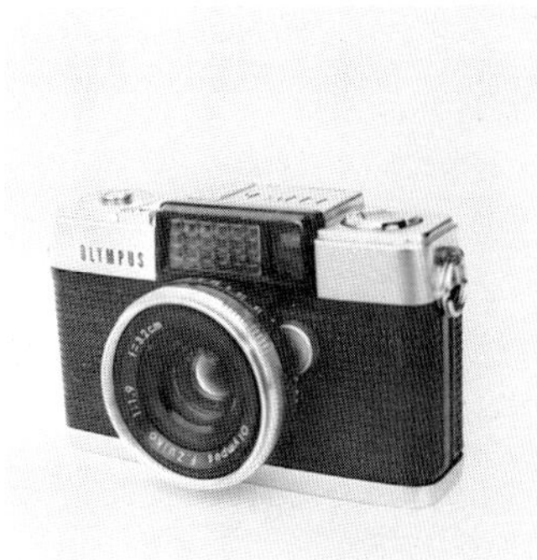

> Q188. 'Amourette'
... An early 35 mm. camera for 50 exposures 24 * 33 mm on cine film carried in a cassette.
The film was transported by a plate with sprung claws which was moved by pulling a rod at the end of the camera. c. 1925

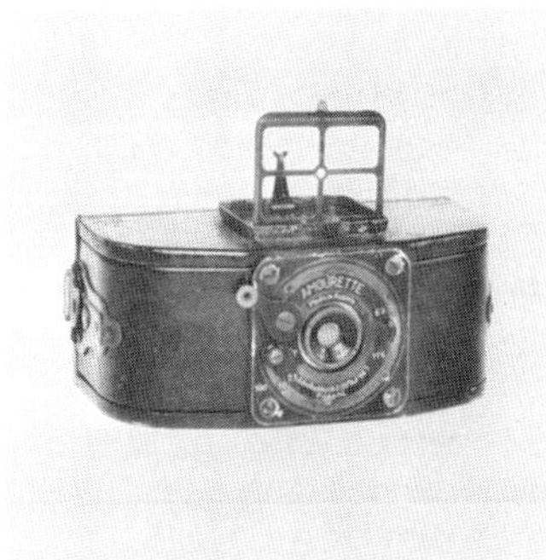

> P361. Tailboard
... PERKEN Son & RAYMENT made a speciality of their tailboard cameras which were of a standard design with no frills but of sound construction. Due to this most of those now sold are in good condition. The small sizes (P362) are the rarer. c. 1880's

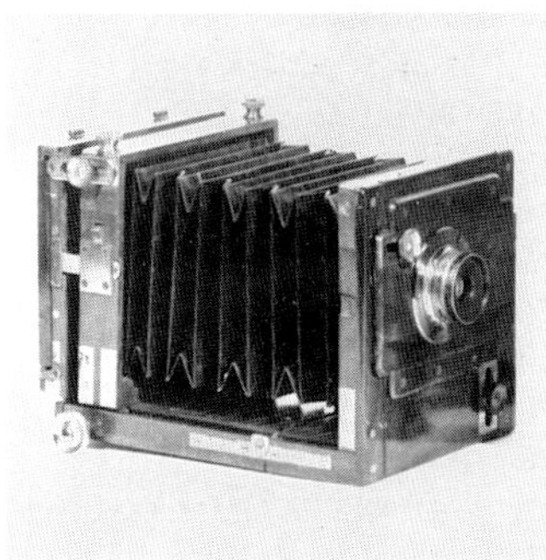

Ref	Name	Data	Average Condition Price Range £	$
PHOTO SERVICE SOCY. (England)				
P364	Field 1/2 plate	**	130-160	220-260
PIGNONS (Switzerland)				
Q190	'Alpa models 5 and 6' S.L.R.	**	170-200	280-340
Q191	'Alpa Prisma' S.L.R.	*	a. 85	a. 150
Q192	'Alpa Reflex 9d' S.L.R.	**	300-360	500-600
PLAUBEL (Frankfurt)				
P365	'Makina' 6.5 * 9 cm	*****	110-120	190-220
R385	'Makinette'strut (16 on 127)	*	a. 460	a. 800
POLAROID (USA)				
> S48	'SX70' S.L.R.	***	30-35	50-60
PRINZ (Hong Kong)				
Q193	'Pilot E'	pcc	5-10	9-18
PURMA (London)				
R386	'Purma Plus' or 'Special'	pcc	8-15	13-25
RAY (Rochester N.Y.)				
P366	'Hand & Stand 5 * 4 in.	**	55-65	95-120
RECTAFLEX (Italy)				
Q194	'Rectaflex' (single lens)	***	130-160	220-260
Q195	'Rectaflex' (3 lens turret)	*	a. 650	a. 1100
REDDING (London)				
> R387	'Luzo' box detective	****	600-750	1100-1300
REID & SIGRIST (Leicester)				
> Q196	'Reid' (Leica copies)	****	140-170	240-280
RENTALL (Birmingham)				
P367	Tailboard 1/2 plate	*	a. 50	a. 90
REVERE (Boston Mass.)				
Q197	'Revere' stereo c.r.f.	*	a. 30	a. 55
REYNOLDS & BRANSON (Leeds)				
P368	Tailboard Meagher 5 * 7in	*	a. 80	a. 140
RICHARD (Paris)				
P369	'Glyphoscope' 45 * 107 mm	***	45-55	80-100
P370	'Verascope' 45 * 107 mm	*****	60-65	100-110
Q198	'Veriscope 40' 35mm stereo	*	a. 260	a. 460
S49	'Taxiphot'auto stereo viewer	***	170-200	280-340

> S48. 'POLAROID SX70'

... A highly innovative instant camera c.1972 wich was not only a flat folding single lens reflex focussing down to below one foot but used a non-peel instant filmpack for daylight development. The SX70 was powered by a battery in the film pack.

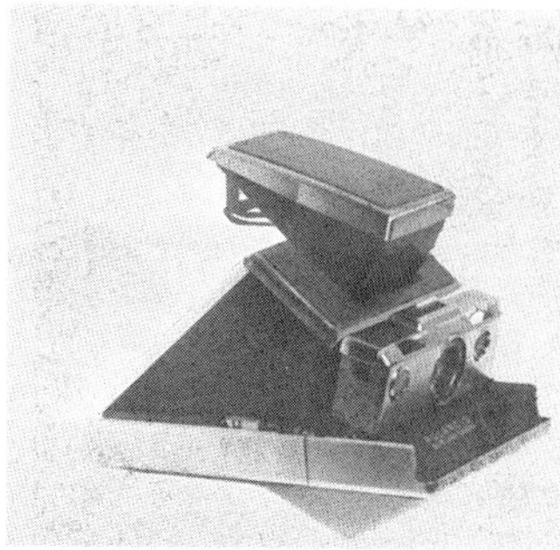

> R387. 'Luzo'

... Patented by H.J.Redding in 1888 this rollfilm box camera was made by J. ROBINSON & Sons of London from 1889 and then by REDDING & GYLES from 1899. The original took 70 mm. pictures on Kodak film; later ones took up to 121 * 165 mm. rectangular frames.

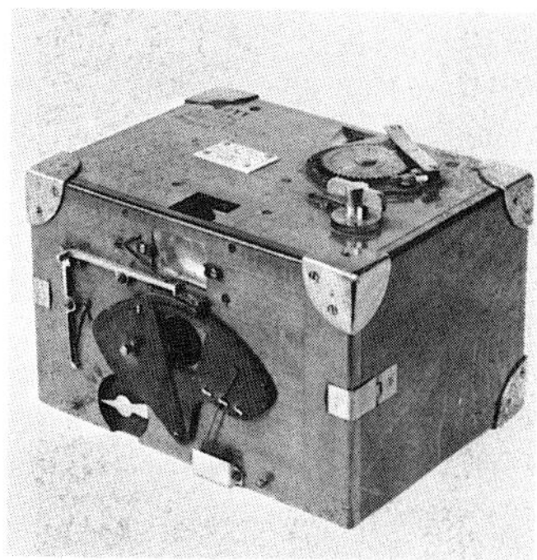

> Q196. 'Reid'

... The post WW2 period saw a spate of cameras copying or closely modelled upon the Leica. In England REID & SIGRIST made precise copies of several versions numbering them :- 1 (without rangefinder); 1a (without viewfinder); 2 (without slow speeds) and 3 (with sync.).

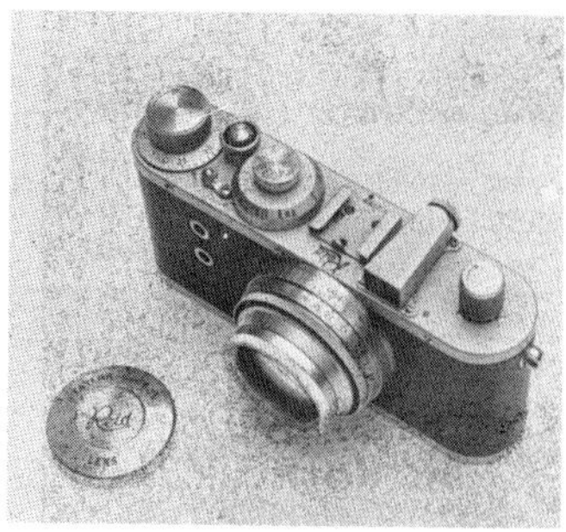

RIETZSCHEL (Munich)

Ref	Name	Data	Average Condition Price Range £	$
P371	'Clack' folding pl.9 * 12 cm	**	25-30	45-55
P372	'Cosmo-Clack'stereo 45 * 107	**	110-130	190-240
RIKEN OPTICAL (Tokyo)				
Q199	'Ricoh' c.r.f. cameras	pcc	20-40	35-70
Q200	'Ricolet' (non rangefinder)	pcc	10-20	18-35
R388	'Ricohflex' 4 * 4 cm T.L.R.	*	a. 18	a. 30
R389	'Ricohmatic' 6 * 6 cm T.L.R.	**	18-20	30-35
S50	'Steky' sub-min. 16 mm	****	60-75	110-130
ROBINSON E /ERAC (London)				
S51	'Erac' pistol (see Merlin)	***	140-170	240-300
ROBINSON J (London)				
P373	'Boys Own' field 1/4 plate	*	a. 40	a. 70
P374	Field 1/1 plate	*	a. 40	a. 70
P375	Tailboard 1/2 plate	*	a. 110	a. 190
ROCHESTER CAMERA (New York)				
P376	'Poco' or 'Cycle Poco' H & S	***	55-65	95-120
P377	'Stereo Poco'	*	a. 140	a. 240
ROCHESTER OPT./E.K.C (New York)				
P378	'Premo' Hand and Stand	****	45-55	80-95
P379	'Long Focus Premo'	**	130-160	220-260
P380	'New Model Improved' 5 * 8 in	*	a. 60	a. 110
P381	'Pony Premo' Hand and Stand	***	60-75	110-130
R390	'Premo No 00 Cartridge' box	**	60-75	110-130
R391	'Premoette' folding	**	17-20	30-35
R392	'Premoette Junior' folding	pcc	10-20	18-35
RODENSTOCK (Munich)				
P382	Folding plate cameras	pcc	10-20	18-35
R393	'Clarovid' c.r.f.	*	a. 55	a. 95
R394	'Ysella' c.r.f.	**	30-35	50-60
ROKUOH-SHA (Japan)				
R395	'Echo' folding strut	*	a. 35	a. 60
ROSS (London)				
P383	'Century' 5 * 7 in. field	*	a. 90	a. 160
P384	Field 1/2 plate	**	75-90	130-160
P385	Folding wet plate 12 * 10 in.	*	a. 380	a. 650
P386	Sliding-box wet plate	**	500-600	850-1000

Ref	Name	Data	Average Condition Price Range £	$
P387	Single lens reflex 1/4 pl.	*	a. 25	a. 45
P388	Tailboard 1/1 plate	**	70-85	120-150
P389	Tailboard transitional	**	550-650	950-1200
> P390	Twin lens reflex 1/4 plate	***	170-200	280-340
P391	Twin lens reflex 5 * 4 in.	**	320-400	550-650
ROSS-ENSIGN see HOUGHTON				
ROUCH (London)				
> P392	'Eureka' detective magazine	***	200-240	340-420
P393	'Patent Portable' 1/2 pl field	*	a. 160	a. 280
P394	Tailboard 5 * 7 mono/stereo	*	a. 120	a. 220
P395	Wet plate sliding-box	*	a. 480	a. 850
ROYALTY (England)				
P396	Field 1/2 plate	**	65-80	110-130
SAKURA (Japan)				
S52	'Petal' sub-miniature	**	140-170	240-300
SALEX (London) see also P330 page 82.				
P397	Field 1/2 plate	*	a. 80	a. 140
P398	Strut folding fps 1/4 pl.	**	65-80	110-130
P399	Strut folding 9 * 12 cm	*	a. 25	a. 45
P400	Single lens reflex 6.5 * 9 cm	**	25-30	45-55
P401	Tailboard 1/1 plate	**	40-50	70-85
R396	Folding early rollfilm	*	a. 40	a. 70
SANDERS & CROWHURST (Brighton)				
P402	'Birdland' S.L.R. 5 * 4 in.	*	a. 150	a. 260
SANDERSON see HOUGHTON				
SANDS HUNTER (London)				
P403	'Imperial' field 1/2 plate	**	85-100	140-170
P404	'Imperial' tailb'd 10 * 12in	**	75-90	130-160
P405	Stereo tailboard 1/2 plate	**	180-220	320-400
P406	Tailboard 1/2 plate	**	110-130	190-240
P407	Tailboard 5 * 7in Meagher type	*	a. 160	a. 280
SANWA/MYCRO CAMERA (Japan)				
> S53	'Mycro 111a' sub-miniature	pcc	15-30	25-50
SARABAR (Goslar)				
Q201	'Finetta'	pcc	8-15	13-25
Q202	'Finetta Super'	pcc	10-20	18-35

> P390. ROSS T.L.R.

... There are two versions of this Twin Lens Reflex which is a tall box style camera with an ingenious double rack focussing system. The first C.1890 has twin double doors opening outwards; the later has a single door hinged to lie flat against the body.

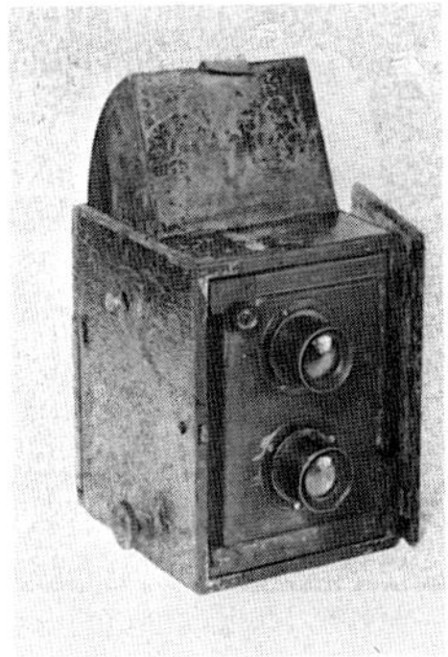

> P392. 'Eureka'

... A sliding box detective camera c.1888 usually of polished mahogany finish but the one shown is hide covered. A roller blind shutter wound by a key was used. It was fitted with a magazine plate changer at the back for 8 * 8 cm. or 1/4 plates.

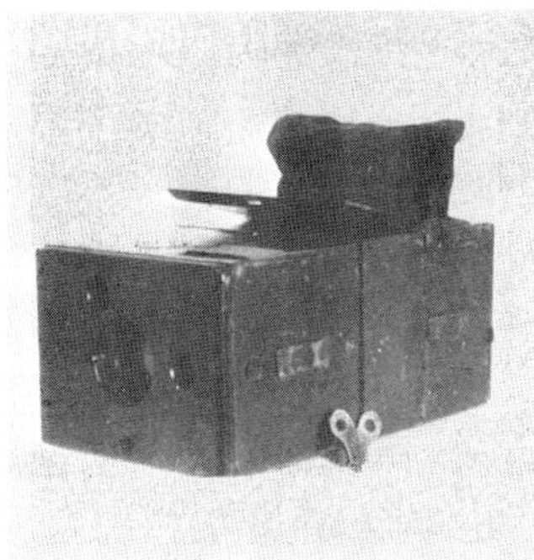

> S53. 'Mycro 111a'

... A Japanese c.1950 sub-miniature of superior construction to that of the 'Hit' types which it resembles. It had a three speed shutter and four lens stops. More expensive is an outfit including tripod with adaptor and e.r.c with pouch for lens hood and filter.

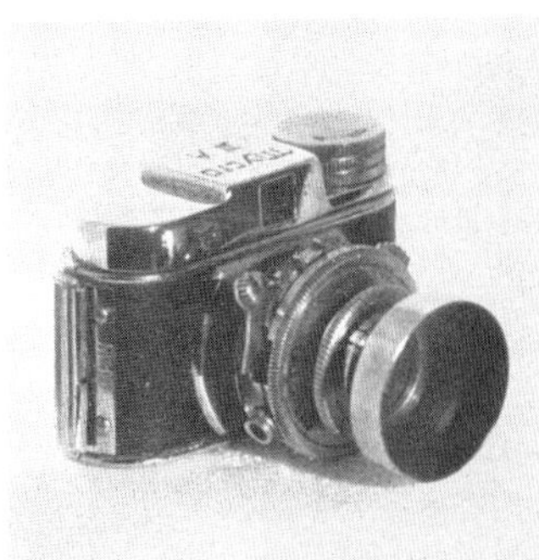

Ref	Name	Data	Average Condition Price Range £	$
SAWYER (Germany/Portland)				
Q203	'Viewmaster' (f2.8 Trinars)	**	70-85	120-150
S.C.A.T (Rome)				
> S54	'Scat' sub-miniature	***	70-85	120-150
SCHUNEMAN & EVANS (St Paul)				
P408	'Lightning' Hand & Stand	*	a. 50	a. 90
SCORER (England)				
P409	Field 10 * 8 in	*	a. 110	a. 190
SECAM (Paris)				
S55	'Stylophot' fountain-pen 16 mm	*	a. 45	a. 80
S.E.M (France)				
Q204	'Kim' (simple 35mm)	pcc	5-10	9-18
R397	'Semflex' T.L.R.	**	14-17	25-30
SHACKMAN (London)				
Q205	Bulk recording cameras	***	35-45	65-80
SHAW H.E/UTILITY Mfg. (USA)				
R398	'Minicam' 16 on 127	pcc	8-15	13-25
SHEW (London)				
P410	'Eclipse' strut 1/4 plate	****	110-130	190-240
> P411	'Xit' strut	*****	95-110	170-190
SHOWA OPTICAL (Japan)				
Q206	'Leotax 1' (Leica 111A copy)	*	a. 85	a. 150
S56	'Gemflex' sub-min. T.L.R 16mm	**	170-200	280-340
SIMMON Bros. (New York)				
R399	'Koni Omega Rapid' press	*	a. 40	a. 70
SINCLAIR (London)				
P412	'Una' Hand & Stand 6.5 * 9 cm	****	240-300	420-500
P413	'Una' Hand & Stand 1/4 pl	*	a. 380	a. 650
> P414	'Una' Hand & Stand tropical	***	550-650	950-1200
P415	'Una' Hand & Stand postcard	*	a. 280	a. 500
P416	'Una Traveller' (aluminium)	*	a. 2600	a. 4600
R400	'Una Traveller' box	**	140-170	240-300
SIRIO (Florence)				
Q207	'Elettra' (Leica 1 copy)	*	a. 60	a. 110
SOENNECKEN (Munich)				
P417	Field 7 * 5 in.	*	a. 60	a. 110

> S54. 'Scat'
... A c.1950 very small sub-miniature camera. The winding knob underneath doubled as the shutter release when rotated in the opposite direction. Single speed shutter and f3.5 lens. Usually found in a leather case which also contains a yellow and a green filter.

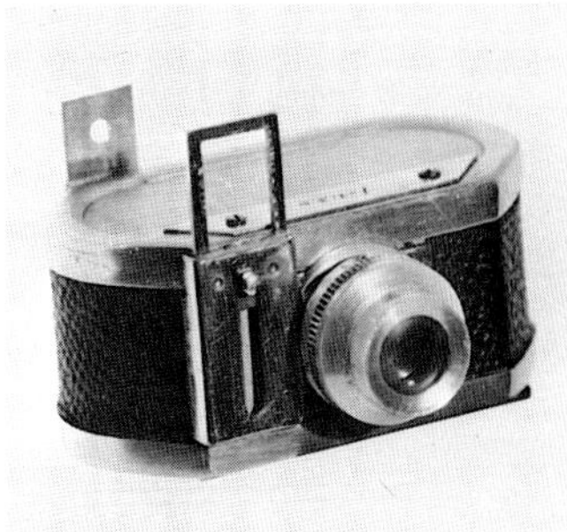

> P411. 'Xit'
... A strut camera with the front supported by flat full width wooden door struts. It was made in variations of finish including an aluminium bound version and a 1/2 plate swing back with tripod adaptor plate.
From c. 1895.

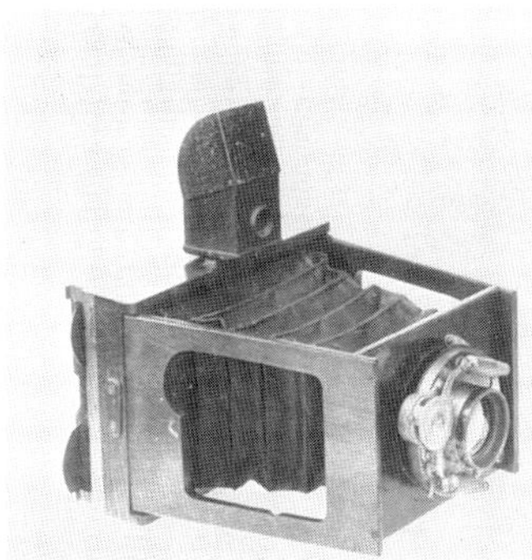

> P414. 'Una' tropical
... This model is probably the most attractive of the 'Una' hand and stand cameras. Highly polished hardwood with brass bound corners put it into the luxury class of 'Una' cameras (1904-30) which were themselves considered the acme of all hand and stands.

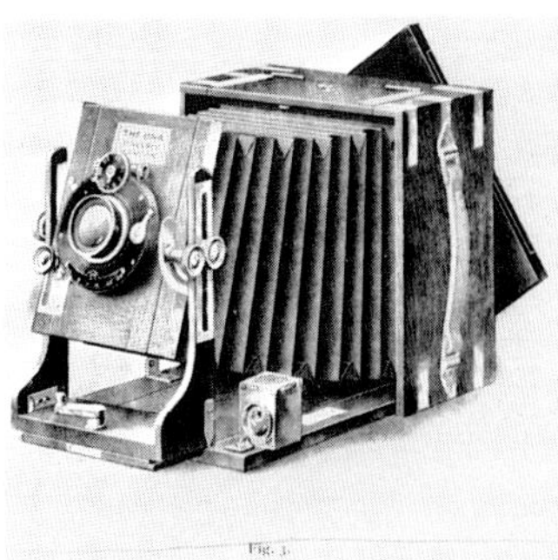

Fig. 3.
Teak and Brass-bound Tropical "Una."

Ref	Name	Data	Average Condition Price Range £	$
SOHO see APEM and MARION				
SMEDLEY (England)				
P418	Field 12 * 10 ins.	*	a. 190	a. 340
SOLOMAN & GRANT (England)				
S57	Magnesium lamp flash unit	*	a. 400	a. 700
SPEICH (Genoa)				
Q208	'Speich' stereo 10 * 12 mm.	*	a. 480	a. 850
SPICER (England)				
P419	Folding wet plate 1/1 plate	**	170-200	280-340
P420	Studio camera 1/1 plate	*	a. 95	a. 170
SPIROTECHNIQUE (France)				
Q209	'Calypso' underwater camera	*	a. 160	a. 280
STANDARD (Birmingham)				
> R401	Box cameras (various)	**	5-6	9-11
STANLEY (England)				
P421	Tailboard 1/2 plate	*	a. 170	a. 300
STEGEMAN (Berlin)				
P422	Stereo strut 3 1/4 * 6 3/4 in	*	a. 180	a. 320
STEREOSCOPIC Co see LONDON STEREO				
STEINHEIL (Munich)				
Q210	'Casca' (viewfinder 35mm)	**	70-85	120-150
STIRN (Berlin)				
> P423	'Waistcoat' camera	***	500-600	850-1000
R402	'America' 7.5 * 10 cm.	*	a. 2600	a. 4600
SUFIZE & MOLITOR (Paris)				
P424	One-shot 3-colour process	*	a. 300	a. 550
SUGAYA (Japan)				
> S58	'Rubix' sub-miniature 16mm	**	40-50	70-85
SUTER (Basle)				
P425	Hand & Stand 1/2 plate	*	a. 120	a. 220
SUTTON/ROSS (London)				
P426	Wet pl.panoramic (water lens)	*	a. 6000	a. 10500
SWINDEN & EARP (England)				
P427	'Magazine' 1/4 plate	**	45-55	80-100
TAIYODO (Japan)				
S59	'Vestkam' sub-miniature 16 mm	**	35-45	65-80

> R401. STANDARD boxes
... In the 1930's this company made a range of both conventional Brownie style boxes and some more novel ones such as the 'Kenilworth' illustrated. They were frequently named after towns including the 'Warwick' and the 'Conway'.

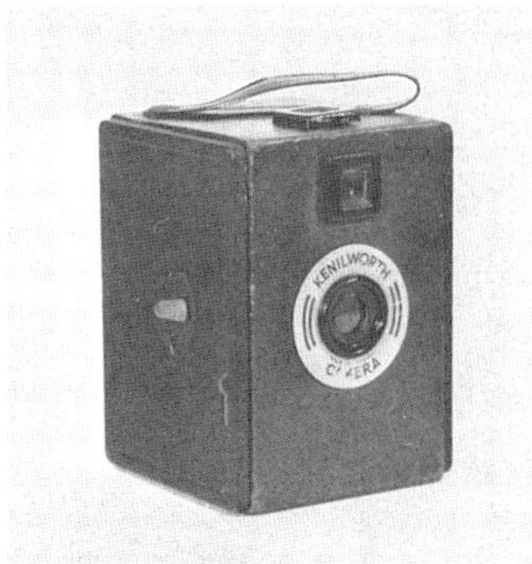

> P423. 'Waistcoat' camera
... A curious detective camera designed by R.D.Gray in 1885/1886 to be worn by gentlemen under the waistcoat (or Vest in the U.S.A.) with the lens pretending to be a button. Several versions were made for circular octagonal or square plates.

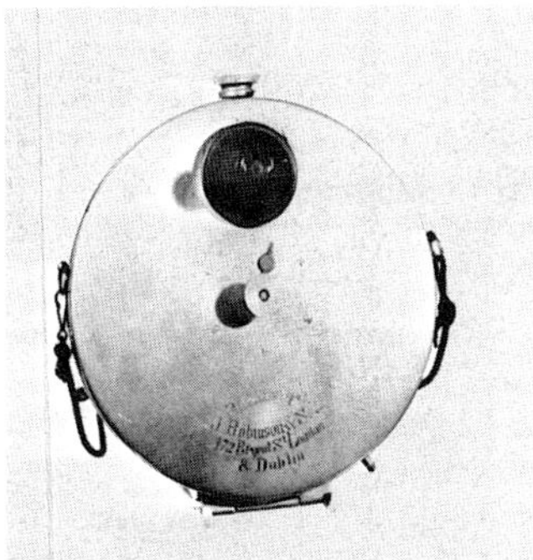

> S58. 'Rubix'
... Like the Mycro 111A (Ref. S53 page.92) a better than usual Japanese 16 mm. sub-miniature. Solidly made of what appears to be stainless steel with a f3.5 lens stopping down to f16 and an exposure counter with double exposure prevention lock. c. 1950.

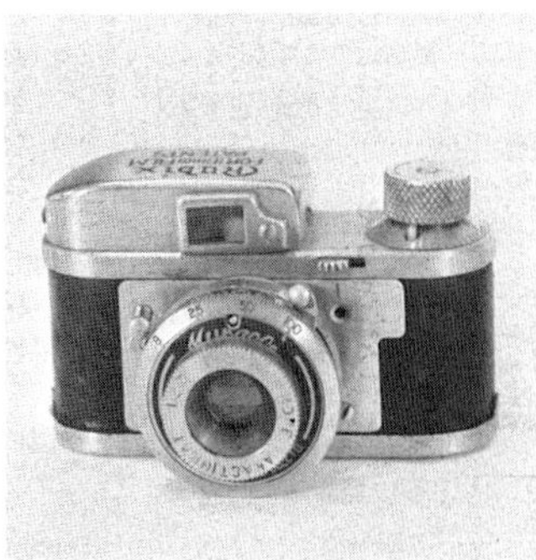

TALBOT & EAMER (Blackburn)

Ref	Name	Data	Average Condition Price Range £	$
P428	Detective 1/4 plate	*	a. 190	a. 340
P429	Field 1/2 plate	*	a. 70	a. 120
P430	'The Talmer' magazine camera	*	a. 70	a. 120
TANAKA (Japan)				
Q211	'Tanack' (Leica 111B copy)	*	a. 80	a. 140
TAYLORS DRUG (London)				
P431	'The Guildford' field 1/4 pl.	*	a. 90	a. 160
P432	'The Initial' field 1/2 pl.	*	a. 70	a. 120
TELLA (London)				
P433	Field 1/2 plate	*	a. 95	a. 170
THIRD DIMENSION see BELL & HOWELL				
THORNTON PICKARD (Altrincham)				
P434	'Aerial Camera Type C'	*	a. 1700	a. 3000
P435	'College' field 1/4 or 1/2 pl	***	85-100	140-170
P436	'Duplex Reflex'	**	45-55	80-100
P437	'Duplex Reflex' tropical	*	a. 900	a. 1600
P438	Field 1/2 pl (various)	*****	110-120	190-200
P439	'Folding Ruby' 1/4 plate	**	70-85	120-150
P440	'Imperial Triple Extn' field	****	90-100	150-170
> P441	'Imperial Pocket" folding	pcc	15-30	25-50
P442	'Limit' falling plate V.P.	*	a. 700	a. 1200
P443	'Nimrod Automan' H & S	**	70-85	120-150
P444	'Ruby' field 1/1 plate	*	a. 130	a. 220
> P445	'Ruby Horizontal' 6 * 9 cm.	*	a. 90	a. 160
P446	'Ruby Speed' 4.5 * 6 cm.	**	2300-2800	4000-4900
P447	'Ruby de luxe' S.L.R. trop.	*	a. 650	a. 1100
P448	Single lens reflex	*****	50-55	85-95
P449	Single lens reflex tropical	**	850-1000	1400-1700
R403	'Hythe' gun camera type G3	*	a. 120	a. 220
> R404	'MK 3H' gun camera 4.5 * 6cm	***	180-220	320-400
R405	'Rubyette No1' rf/pl S.L.R.	*	a. 85	a. 150
R406	'Stereo Puck' 6 * 8.5 cm.	****	40-50	70-85
TOAKOKI (Tokyo)				
R407	'Gelto' folding (16 on 127)	**	50-60	85-100
TOPCON (Tokyo)				
P235	'Horseman' press 6.5 * 9 cm	*	a. 240	a. 440

> P441. 'Imperial Pocket' ... Folding plate cameras by THORNTON-PICKARD c.1920 of heavy and rather cumbersome construction.
They are found most frequently in 1/4 plate size and may be either single extension or double extension rack focussing.

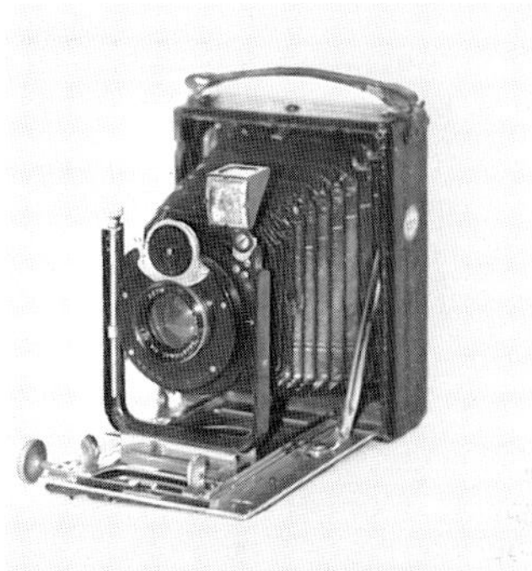

> P445. 'Ruby Horizontal' ... One of the 'Ruby' series of THORNTON-PICKARD cameras this attractive S.L. R. was a compact version for horizontal 6 * 9 cm. pictures.
The 'Ruby Horizontal' had a non-reversing back and spring loaded square viewing hood. c.1920's.

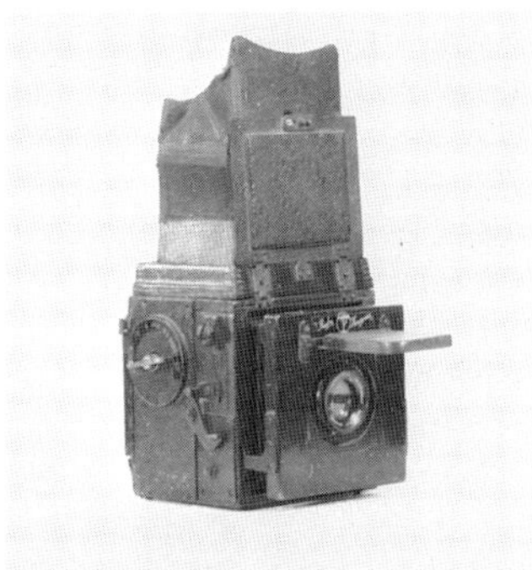

> R404. 'Mark 3H' gun camera ... The 'Hythe' gun camera was made from 1915 to 1925 as a British aircrew training camera. It has the look of an adapted Lewis machine gun of the period. The image formed by the 300 mm. f8 lens was recorded on rollfilm when the gun trigger was pulled.

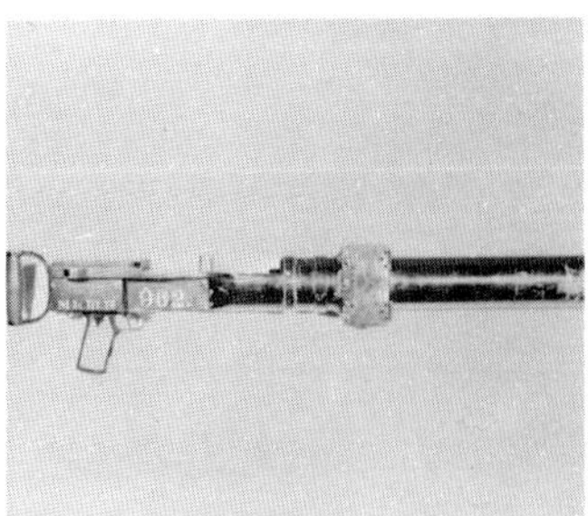

TOPCON (Tokyo)(cont'd)

Ref	Name	Data	Average Condition Price Range £	$
Q212	'Minion 35' (viewfinder 35mm)	*	a. 15	a. 25
Q213	'Topcon RE Super'	*	a. 140	a. 240
TOWER /SEARS ROEBUCK (U.S.A.)				
Q214	'Tower' ('Nicca' Leica copy)	**	80-100	140-170
TOYO (Tokyo)				
S60	'Mighty' sub-min. telephoto	*	a. 40	a. 70
TROTTER J (England)				
P450	Field 1/2 plate	*	a. 65	a. 110
TYLAR (Birmingham)				
P451	'Featherweight' field 1/4 pl	*	a. 80	a. 140
P452	'Pocket Titbit' strut 6 * 9	*	a. 170	a. 300
P453	'Stereoscopic Titbit'	*	a. 150	a. 260
ULCA CAMERA (Pittsburg)				
> S61	'Ulca' sub-miniature 16mm	**	18-20	30-35
S62	'Ulca'(red finish) 16 mm	*	a. 55	a. 95
UNDERWOOD (Birmingham)				
P454	'Club' field 1/2 plate	**	85-100	140-170
P455	'Instanto' tailboard	****	70-85	120-150
UNITED OPTICAL INST (England)				
> S63	'Merlin' sub-min.	*	a. 55	a. 95
UNIVERSAL (New York)				
Q215	'Mercury' 1/2 frame	pcc	20-40	35-70
Q216	'Univex AF..' compact	*	a. 45	a. 80
> S64	'Minute 16' or 'Tynar' 16mm	**	30-35	50-60
USSR/KMZ (also see page 50)				
S38	'Narcis' sub-min. S.L.R.	*	a. 220	a. 420
Q217	'Horizont' panoramic	****	220-260	380-460
R408	'Moskwa' (Super-Ikonta copy)	**	25-30	45-55
VALSTS E.F (Riga & see MINOX)				
S65	'Minox' (original type)	***	280-340	480-600
VAN NECK see PEELING & VAN NECK				
VARIMEX (Poland)				
Q218	'Alfa-2' (vertical format)	***	30-35	50-60
VEGA (Geneva)				
P457	'Vega' auto-change 1/4pl.mag.	*	a. 360	a. 650

> S61. 'Ulca'
... An American designed sub-miniature also made in England and Germany c. 1935.
The meniscus lens and single speed shutter appear to be attached to the body casting almost as an afterthought.

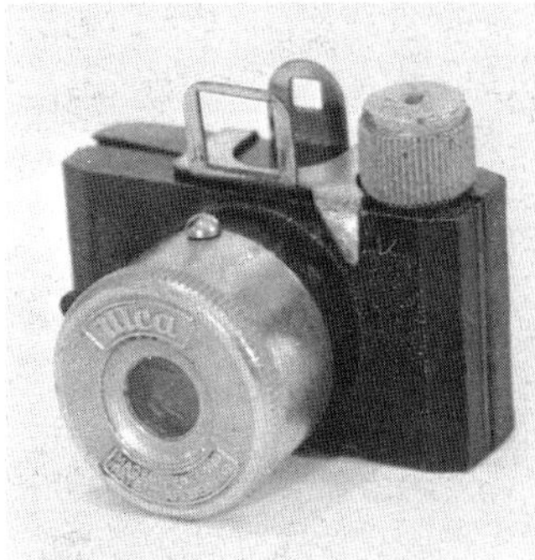

> S63. 'Merlin'
... A simple rather crudely made cast metal sub-miniature for 20 * 20 mm pictures on special rollfilm.
Usually found in a black finish but coloured versions exist. c.1936.
An adapted version is used in the 'Erac' pistol camera.

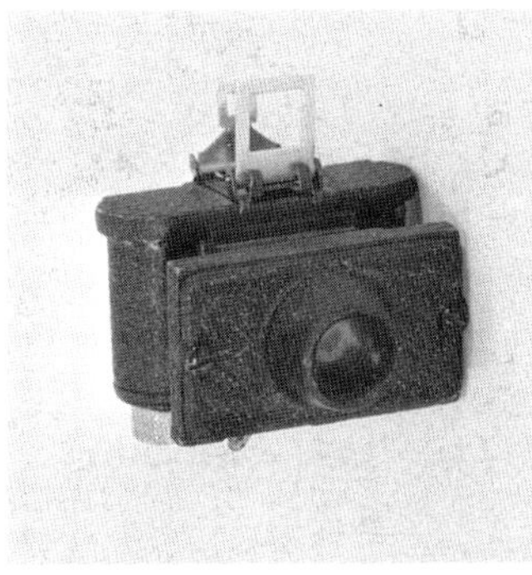

> S64. 'Minute 16'/'Tynar'
... These two 16 mm. sub-miniatures are grouped here for commonality of design and price. The 'Minute 16' was made in New York and the 'Tynar' in Los Angeles. Both look like small cine cameras.

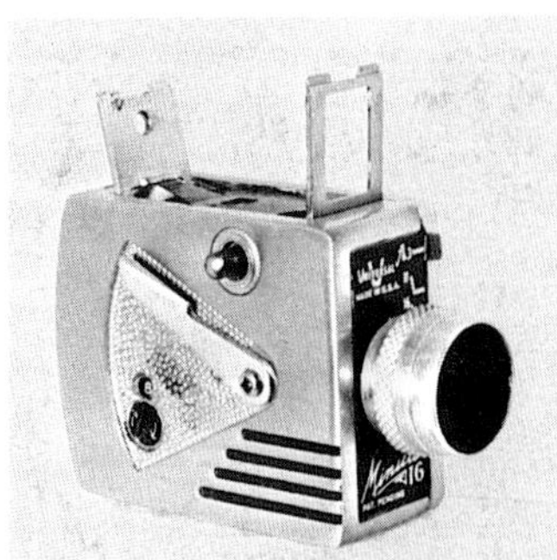

Ref	Name	Data	Average Condition Price Range £	$
VENA (Amsterdam)				
R410	'Vena-Box' (220 film)	pcc	8-15	13-25
VOIGTLANDER (Braunschweig)				
P458	'Alpin' stereo panoram folding	*	a. 500	a. 900
P459	'Avus' folding plate	pcc	10-20	18-35
P460	'Bijou' S.L.R. 4.5 * 6 cm.	*	a. 1200	a. 2100
> P461	'Bergheil' 4.5 * 6 cm.	**	140-170	240-300
P462	'Bergheil' 6.5 * 9 cm	pcc	30-60	55-110
P463	'Heliar' S.L.R. 9 * 12 cm.	*	a. 35	a. 60
P464	'Stereoflektoscop' 45 * 107	***	150-180	260-320
P465	'Vag' folding	**	18-20	30-35
Q219	'Bessamatic' S.L.R.	***	75-90	130-160
Q220	'Prominent' c.r.f 35mm	**	40-50	70-85
Q221	'Ultramatic' S.L.R. outfit	*	a. 240	a. 420
Q222	'Vitessa' c.r.f. folding	***	25-30	45-55
Q223	'Vitessa N' c.r.f folding	pcc	30-60	55-110
> Q224	'Vitessa T' c.r.f. rigid	*	a. 60	a. 110
Q225	'Vito' folding 35mm cameras	pcc	10-20	18-35
Q226	'Vito B' rigid body	pcc	15-30	25-50
Q227	'Vito 111' c.r.f. folding	pcc	30-60	55-110
Q228	'Vitomatic'	**	18-20	30-35
R411	Folding 6.5 * 11 cm (116)	pcc	15-30	25-50
R412	Folding V.P.	pcc	15-30	25-50
R413	'Baby Bessa' (16 on 120)	pcc	20-40	35-70
R414	'Bessa' (f3.5 Voigtar/Skopar)	pcc	15-30	25-50
R415	'Bessa' (f7.7 Voigtar)	pcc	8-15	13-25
R416	'Bessa' (f3.5 Heliar)	pcc	20-40	35-70
R417	'Bessa R F' c.r.f. (pre-war)	pcc	30-60	55-110
R418	'Bessa 11' c.r.f. (post-war)	**	140-170	240-300
> R419	'Brilliant' (non-focussing)	pcc	8-15	13-25
R420	'Brilliant' (focussing)	pcc	15-30	25-50
R421	'Inos 11' c.r.f.	**	25-30	45-55
R422	'Perkeo 1 or 11' (12 on 120)	pcc	8-15	13-25
R423	'Perkeo' (pre-set focussing)	**	80-100	140-170
R424	'Prominent' folding c.r.f	****	220-260	380-460
R425	'Superb' T.L.R.	****	85-100	140-170

> P461. 'Bergheil'

... Illustrated is the diminutive V.P. (4.5 * 6 cm) version of the Bergheil range of double extension folding plate cameras. The lens is an f4.5 80 mm. Heliar. This category does not cover the Luxus coloured model or the rare Tele-Dynar telephoto lens. c.1914.

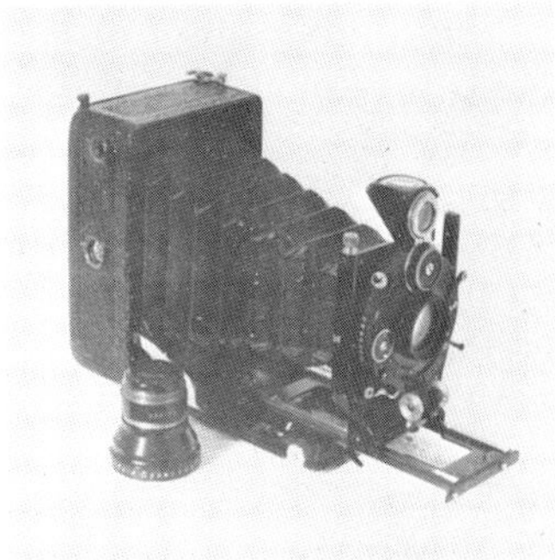

> Q224. 'Vitessa T'

... The folding 'Vitessa's introduced c. 1950 were c.r.f. bellows cameras with Color-Skopar or Ultron lenses in Synchro-Compur shutters.
However the last of the 'Vitessa's' the 'T' model of c. 1957 had a rigid front as illustrated.

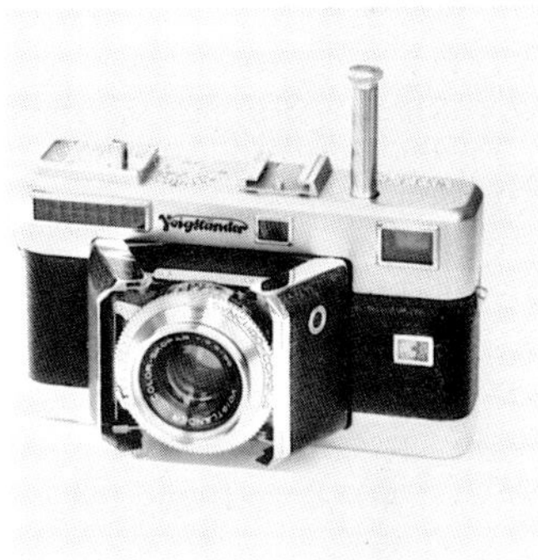

> R419. 'Brilliant'

... An inexpensive and popular Twin Lens Reflex by Voigtlander c. 1933. This category covers the non-focussing versions of the 'Brilliant' which was usually fitted with a Voigtar f7.7 lens.
For the focussing versions see Ref. R420.

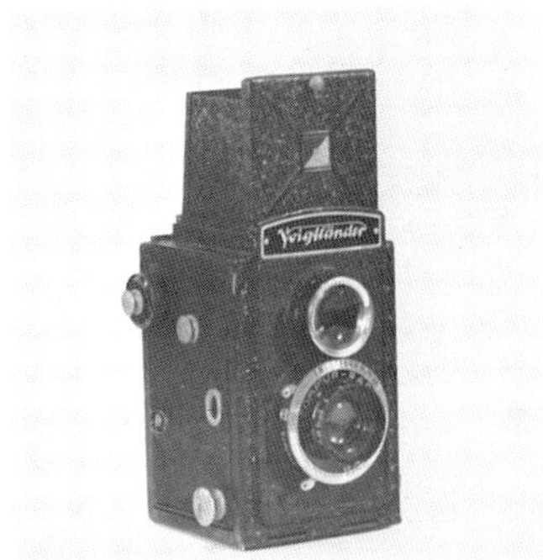

	Ref	Name	Data	Average Condition Price Range £	$
	R426	'Virtus' folding c.r.f.	**	65-80	110-130
	S66	Daguerrotype (replica)	*	a. 950	a. 1700
VOSS (Ulm)					
	Q229	'Diax' rigid body	**	18-20	30-35
WALLER & RILEY (Bolton)					
	P466	Field 1/2 plate	*	a. 85	a. 150
WATKINS ALFRED (England)					
>	S67	'Bee' exposure meter	pcc	8-15	13-25
WATSON (London)					
	P467	'Argus' reflex	**	30-35	50-60
>	P468	'Alpha' H & S 5 * 4 in	***	280-340	480-600
	P469	Field 1/2 plate	**	140-170	240-300
	P470	Field 1/1 plate	***	160-200	280-340
	P471	Field 10 * 8 or 12 * 10 in.	**	120-150	220-260
	P472	Field 15 * 12 in	**	240-300	420-500
	P473	Microscopy camera 1/2 pl.	*	a. 20	a. 35
	P474	Process camera 1/2 plate	*	a. 70	a. 120
	P475	'Stereo Binocular'	*	a. 700	a. 1200
	P476	Studio wet/dry pl. 8 * 8 in.	*	a. 240	a. 420
	P477	Tailboard 5 * 4 to 10 * 12 in	*****	130-150	240-280
	P478	Tailboard 15 * 12 in.	***	180-220	320-400
	P479	'Vanneck' reflex	*	a. 170	a. 300
WELTA (Freital)					
	Q230	'Welti' folding	pcc	15-30	25-50
	Q231	'Weltini' c.r.f.	**	20-25	35-45
	Q232	'Weltix' folding	pcc	10-20	18-35
	R427	'Gucki' folding strut	pcc	15-30	25-50
	R428	'Perfekta' folding T.L.R.	****	90-110	160-200
	R429	'Perle' (16 on 120)	pcc	10-20	18-35
	R430	'Superfekta' fold. T.L.R.	**	240-300	420-500
>	R431	'Welta' folding	*	a. 15	a. 25
	R432	'Weltaflex' T.L.R.	pcc	10-20	18-35
	R433	'Weltur' or 'Weltini'	*	a. 40	a. 70
WEMBLEY (London)					
	R434	'Wembley Sports'	pcc	5-10	9-18

> S67. 'Bee' meter
... The most popular of all 'watch type' tint meters from c. 1902 to 1940 this actinometer used the principle of Alfred Watkins patent of 1890 and sold in vast quantities with various dials. Not included in S67 S67 are the silver Queen Bee or early cylinder meters.

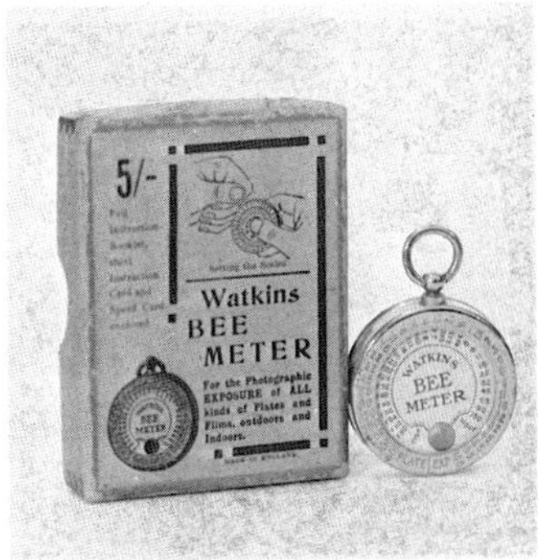

> P468. 'Alpha' H & S
... A very well made English hand & stand camera usually with polished mahogany woodwork and brass fittings as on the model illustrated but also found with a leather covered body. A good example of the camera makers art. First made in 1892.

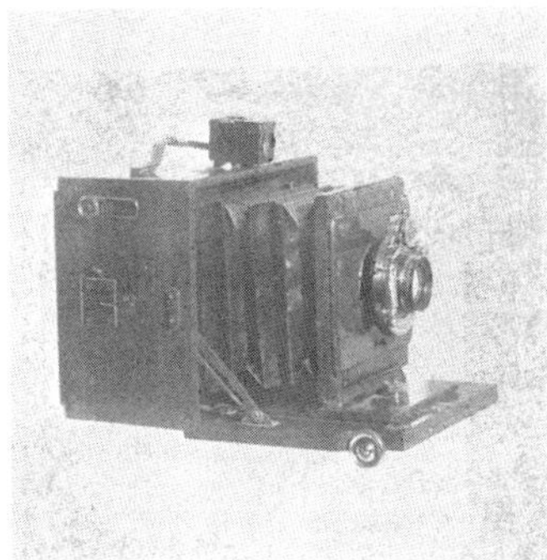

> R431. 'Welta'
... An example of German made folding roll film cameras of the 1930's. Various models for 6 * 6 cm. (12 on 120) or 6 * 9 cm. (8 on 120) with different lens and shutter combinations. Similar in design and price is the 8 or 16 on 120 'Weltax'.

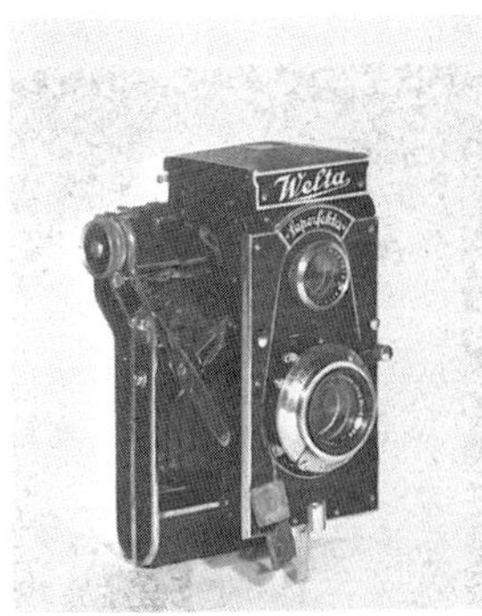

Ref	Name	Data	Average Condition Price Range £	$
WENK (Nuernberg)				
Q233	'Wenka' (Leica copy)	*	a. 120	a. 220
WESTFALISCHER (Germany)				
Q234	'Navex' viewfinder 35mm	*	a. 140	a. 240
WESTON (USA)				
> S68	'Master' etc. earlier meters	pcc	10-20	18-35
S69	'Master' etc. later meters	pcc	15-30	25-50
WHITE D (Milwaukee)				
> Q235	'Stereo Realist'	***	85-100	140-170
Q236	'Stereo Realist' outfit	*	a. 200	a. 360
WHITEHOUSE PRODUCTS (Brooklyn)				
R435	'Beacon' plastic	pcc	5-10	9-18
WILLIAMSON (Reading)				
P480	Pistol camera 6.5 * 9cm.	*	a. 150	a. 260
R436	'G22' gun camera'	*	a. 30	a. 55
R437	'G45' gun camera'	***	17-20	30-35
WILMOT (London)				
P481	Magazine 1/4 plate	*	a. 100	a. 180
WING (Boston Mass.)				
P482	Ferrotype/wet plate studio	*	a. 600	a. 1100
WIRGIN (Wiesbaden)				
> Q237	'Edinex' compact	**	16-20	30-35
Q238	'Edinex' with c.r.f	**	25-30	45-55
Q239	'Edixa' S.L.R.	**	30-35	50-60
Q240	'Edixa Stereo'	***	75-90	130-160
R438	'Klein-Edinex' (16 on 127)	pcc	50-100	90-180
R439	Folding rollfilm 6 * 9 cm.	**	20-25	35-45
WITT (Hamburg)				
Q241	'Iloca Rapid' c.r.f	pcc	8-15	13-25
Q242	'Iloca Stereo' 23 * 24 mm	***	70-85	120-150
Q243	'Iloca Stereo Rapid' c.r.f	*	a. 90	a. 160
WOOD E.G (London)				
P483	Wet plate sliding box	*	a. 400	a. 700
WOOLLEY (Manchester)				
P484	'New Baroness' field 1/2 pl.	*	a. 190	a. 340
WRATTEN & WAINWRIGHT (London)				
P485	'Long Focus Tailboard'	*	a. 240	a. 420

> S68. WESTON meters
... Probably the best known of all photo-electric meters based on the selenium cell made by WESTON from c. 1932.
It was made in many models up to the 'Master V' and 'Euromaster'.

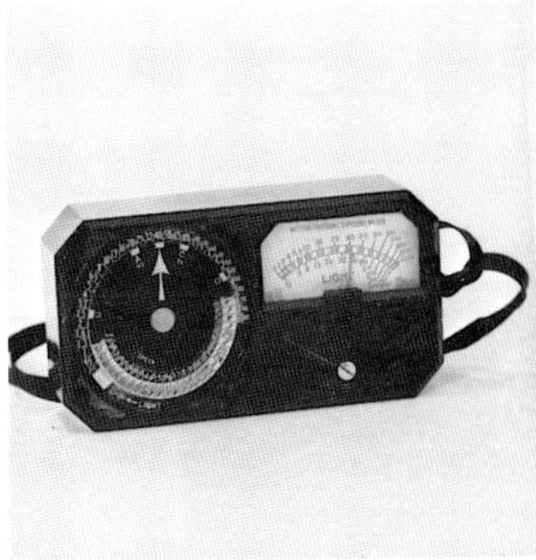

> Q235. 'Stereo Realist'
... A popular 35 mm. stereo camera of 1945 with movable film plane adjusted by the focussing control. The central lens was an optical direct vision finder and a long base coupled rangefinder was fitted. Two models with f3.5 and f2.8 lenses respectively.

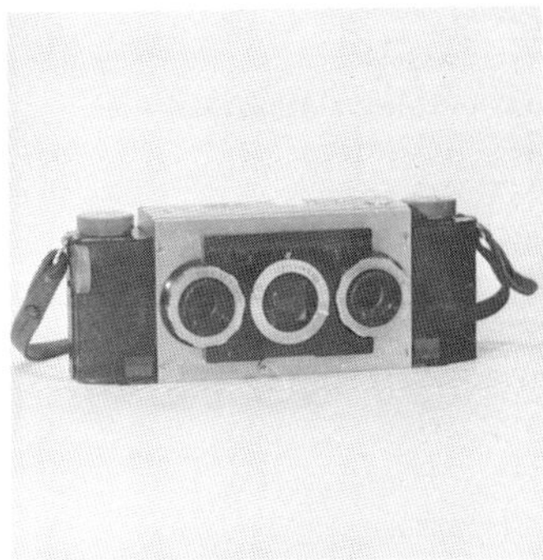

> Q237. 'Edinex' compact
... A range of inexpensive 35 mm. view cameras with collapsible lens on sale from the 1930's to 1950's. Some later models were fitted with rangefinders and with improved lenses having apertures from f2 to f4.5. Also marketed as the ADOX 'Adrette'

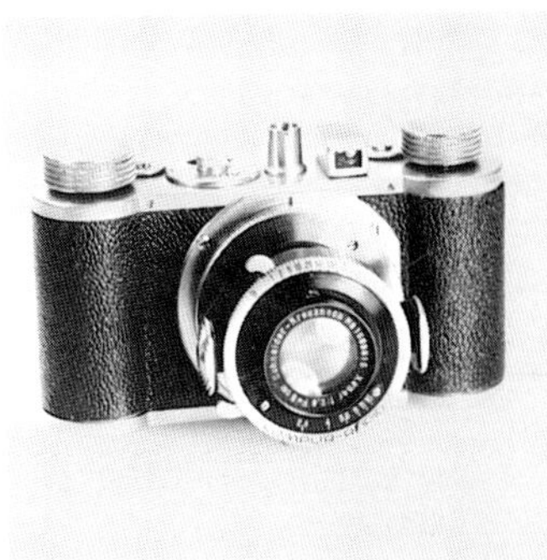

WRATTEN & WAINWRIGHT (London)(cont'd)

Ref	Name	Data	Average Condition Price Range £	$
P486	Tailboard 13 * 18 cm	*	a. 190	a. 340
P487	Tailboard 1/2 plate	**	80-100	140-170
WRAY (London)				
Q244	'Stereo Graphic'	****	55-65	95-120
Q245	'Stereo Graphic' outfit	*	a. 130	a. 220
> Q246	'Wrayflex' S.L.R.	**	90-110	160-200
Q247	'Wrayflex' (& Lustrar 13.5cm)	*	a. 130	a. 220
Q248	'Wrayflex' outfit	*	a. 180	a. 320
WUNSCHE (Dresden)				
R440	Folding rollfilm	**	25-30	45-55
WYNNE G.F (England)				
> S70	'Infallible' exposure meter	**	35-45	65-80
S71	'Infallible' silver model	*	a. 140	a. 240
YAMATO (Tokyo)				
Q249	'Pax' c.r.f.	**	30-35	50-60
YASHICA (Japan)				
Q250	'Mimy' half frame (auto exp.)	pcc	15-30	25-50
Q251	'Penta' S.L.R.	*	a. 18	a. 30
Q252	'Sequelle' (motor-driven)	*	a. 40	a. 70
Q253	'YF' (Leica copy)	**	45-55	80-100
R441	Twin lens reflex 4 * 4 cm	****	35-45	65-80
ZEH (Dresden)				
R442	'Goldi' folding (16 on 127)	**	20-25	35-45
R443	'Zecaflex' folding T.L.R.	**	280-340	480-600
ZEISS CARL JENA/ICA see also 'Werra' page 112.				
P488	'Minimum Palmos'	**	80-100	140-170
P489	'Stereo Palmos' 9 * 12 cm.	*	a. 65	a. 110
P490	'Stereo Palmos' 1/4 pl outfit	*	a. 750	a. 1300
ZEISS IKON (Dresden)				
> Q254	'Contaflex' S.L.R.	****	50-60	90-100
Q255	'Contaflex' T.L.R.	****	460-550	800-950
Q257	'Contaflex' T.L.R. outfit	*	a. 1100	a. 1900
Q258	'Contarex' S.L.R.	***	180-220	320-400
Q259	'Contarex' S.L.R. outfit	**	650-800	1100-1300
Q260	'Contax 1'	*****	160-180	280-300
Q261	'Contax 1' (with sync.sh'tr)	**	40-50	70-85

> Q246. 'Wrayflex'
... Made in England from 1950 to 1954 the first Wrayflex took 40 exposures 24 * 32 mm. on standard length cassettes. It was eventually modified to take standard 24 * 36 mm. exposures. Q 246 does not include the rarer 'Wrayflex 11' with pentaprism finder.

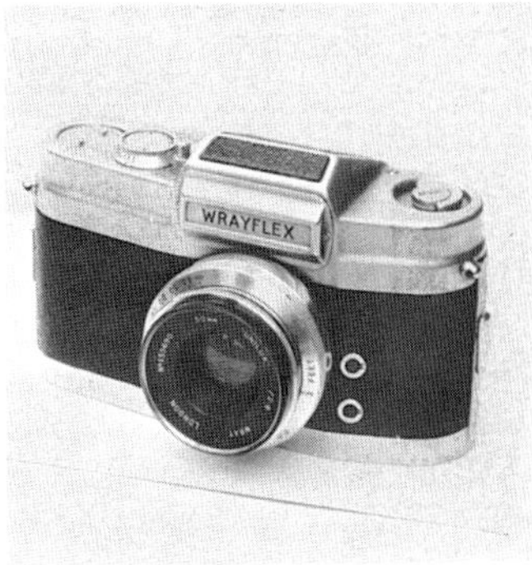

> S70. 'Infallible' meter
... G.F. WYNNE's 'Infallible' meter of 1894 was very similar in design to the WATKINS 'Bee' at Ref.S67 but rather larger. As it was less popular fewer were made and it is now more collectable than the 'Bee'.Two versions only were produced.

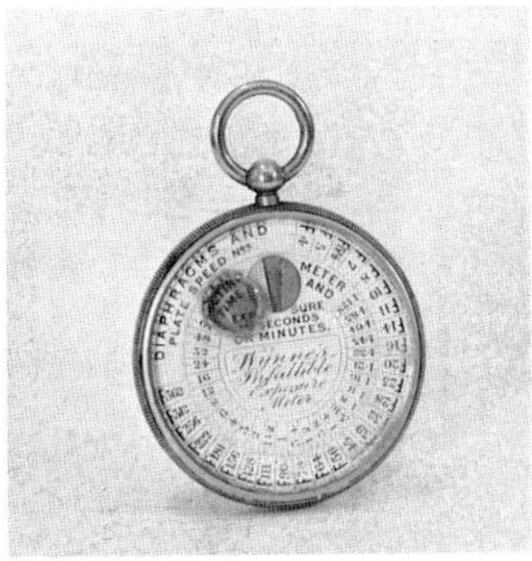

> Q255. 'Contaflex' T.L.R.
... A high quality 35 mm T.L.R. taking a range of interchangeable Zeiss lenses with focal lengths from 35 to 135 mm. Introduced 1935 it was the first camera with a built-in photo-electric exposure meter.
Collectors price very dependant upon condition.

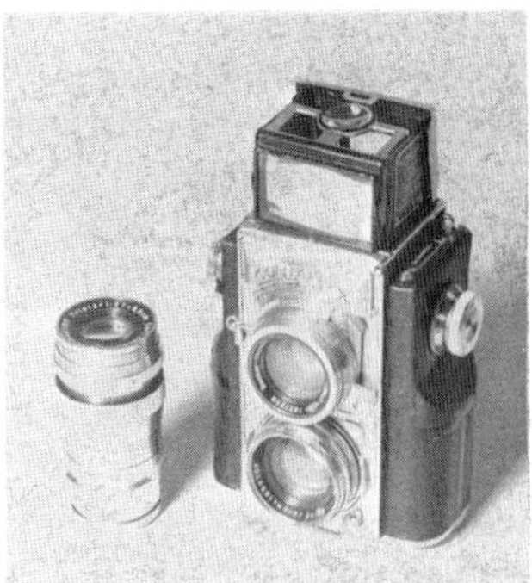

Ref	Name	Data	Average Condition Price Range £	$
Q262	'Contax 1' (AU serial No)	*	a. 340	a. 600
Q263	'Contax 11' (Sonnar f2)	*****	70-80	120-140
Q264	'Contax 11' (Sonnar f1.5)	***	60-75	110-130
Q265	'Contax 11' (Tessar f2.8)	**	50-60	85-100
Q266	'Contax 11' (Tessar 3.5)	**	75-90	130-160
Q267	'Contax 11a' (Sonnar f1.5/2)	**	65-80	110-130
Q268	'Contax 11a' (Tessar f3.5)	*	a. 190	a. 340
Q269	'Contax 111' (Sonnar f1.5)	***	60-75	110-130
Q270	'Contax 111a' (Sonnar f1.5)	***	120-150	220-260
Q271	'Contax 111' (Sonnar f2)	****	70-85	120-140
Q272	'Contax non-rangefinder'	*	a. 600	a. 1100
Q273	'Contessa' c.r.f.	**	35-45	65-80
Q274	'Contina 1' folding	pcc	10-20	18-35
Q275	'Contina 11' (unc.r.f.)	pcc	15-30	25-50
Q276	'Icarex' S.L.R.	*	a. 40	a. 70
Q277	'Nettax' c.r.f.	**	140-170	240-300
Q278	'Super Nettel' folding 35mm	****	150-180	260-320
Q279	'Tenax 1' (24 * 24 mm.)	*	a. 40	a. 70
R444	'Baby Box Tengor'(16 on 127)	pcc	15-30	25-50
R445	'Baby Ikonta' (16 on 127)	***	35-45	65-80
R446	Box cameras (lots)	**	8-10	14-17
R447	'Box Tengor 54/2'	pcc	8-15	13-25
R448	'Box Tengor 54/18'	pcc	10-20	18-35
R449	'Erabox' (8 or 12 on 120)	pcc	8-15	13-25
> R450	'Ikoflex 1 or 11' T.L.R.	****	35-45	65-80
R451	'Ikoflex 111' T.L.R.	**	80-100	140-170
R452	'Ikoflex Favorit 887/16'	*	a. 100	a. 180
R453	'Ikonta' folding	**	14-17	25-30
R454	'Ikonta C' with unc.r.f.	pcc	20-40	35-70
> R455	'Kolibri' (16 on 127)	***	90-110	160-200
R456	'Nettar' folding	pcc	10-20	18-35
> R457	'Super Ikonta' c.r.f.	*****	85-95	150-170
R458	'Super Six' (f2.8 Tessar)	*	a. 65	a. 110

Z.I.also see CONTESSA-NETTEL/Z.I.
Z.I.also see ERNEMANN/Z.I.
Z.I.also see GOERZ/Z.I & ICA/Z.I.

> R450. 'Ikoflex'
... The Ikoflexes were made from 1934 to 1960 and are divided into three price groups.
Ref. R450 covers all the models c.1934 to 1956 except the 111 with the large Albada finder (Ref.R451) 1939 to 40. The 'Favorit' of 1957 to 1960 is at Ref.R452.

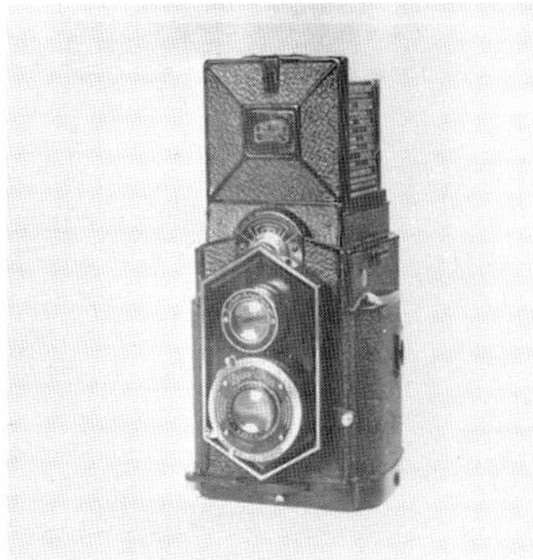

> R455. 'Kolibri'
... A very collectable rollfilm camera of 1930 to 1935 for 16 exposures on 127 film . The lens and shutter are mounted on an extension tube and are most commonly a Novar f4.5 or Tessar f3.5 in Telma or Compur shutter. The higher spec. models fetch a premium price.

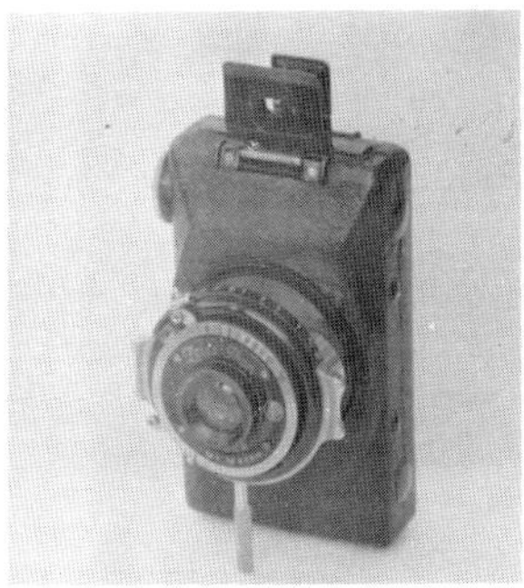

> R457. 'Super Ikonta'
... Probably the high quality rollfilm camera to come most frequently to auction. They were made from 1934 to 1960 in many models and sizes. Those up to 1956 had the characteristic rotating prism rangefinder. Still an eminently usable camera.

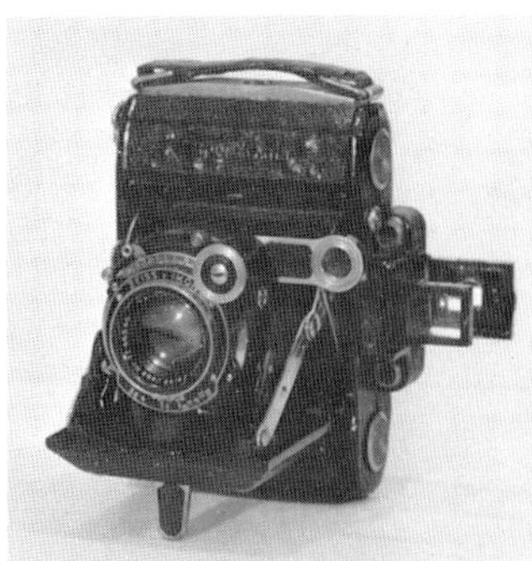

Ref	Name	Data	Average Condition Price Range £	$
ZEISS IKON/PENTACON (Dresden)				
Q280	'Contax D'	**	40-50	70-85
Q281	'Contax E'	*	a. 70	a. 120
Q282	'Contax F'	*	a. 35	a. 60
Q283	'Pentacon F' body only	pcc	8-15	13-25
Q284	'Pentacon FB' S.L.R.	*	a. 45	a. 80
Q285	'Pentacon FM' S.L.R.	*	a. 40	a. 70
Q286	'Pentaflex' S.L.R.	pcc	15-30	25-50
Q287	'Penti' (coloured body)	**	14-17	25-30
Q288	'Pentina'S.L.R.	*	a. 30	a. 55
Q289	'Pentona 11' (simple 35mm)	pcc	5-10	9-18
Q290	'Taxona' (= late Tenax 1)	pcc	20-40	35-70
> Q291	'Werra' (by CARL ZEISS JENA)	pcc	10-20	18-35
Q292	'Werra' (green) " "	pcc	15-30	25-50
Q293	'Werramatic' " "	pcc	15-30	25-50
Q294	'Werra de luxe'(silvered by ?)	*	a. 25	a. 45
ZEISS/YASHICA (Japan)				
Q295	'Contax RTS'	*	a. 240	a. 420
ZENIT see KMZ				
ZENZA (Japan)				
R459	'Bronica' S.L.R. outfit	**	700-850	1200-1500
ZION (Paris)				
P491	'Pocket Z' stereo strut	*	a. 110	a. 190
ZODEL (London)				
P492	Folding plate 9 * 12 cm	**	25-30	45-55
ZORKI see KMZ				
ZULAUF (Switzerland)				
> P493	'Bebe' folding strut V.P.	*	a. 60	a. 110

> Q291. 'Werra'
... The 'Werra' range of cameras by CARL ZEISS JENA were made between 1954 and 1964. The were of innovative design and high quality and are still essentially a users camera. The green finish (Q292) is preferred by collectors to the black.

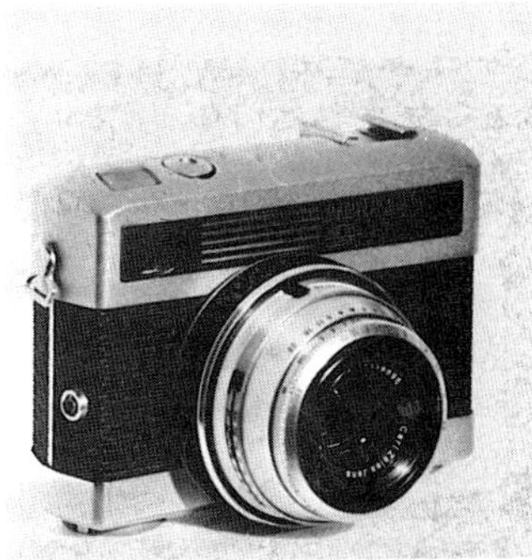

> P493. ZULAUF 'Bebe'
... Predecessor of the ICA 'Bebe' (Ref.P220 page 46) made c.1908 by the Swiss firm which was bought by ICA in 1911. Distinguished from the ICA by the latters Compur shutter and also looking at the two side by side the ZULAUF appears to be upside down!

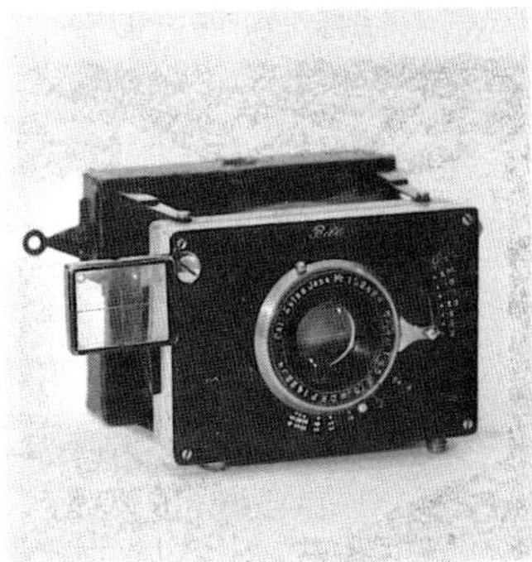

MAKERS

The MAKERS names in this Guide generally follow the relevant auction catalogue entries. In some cases, particularly those of single * entry wood and brass cameras the MAKER quoted is actually that of the dealer, agent or trader whose name is given on the camera name plaque.

Ref	Name	Data	Average Condition Price Range £	$
VARIOUS MAKERS (incl. unknown)				
P494	Boxform (cardboard) V.P.	**	55-65	95-120
P495	Detective cameras	*****	85-95	150-170
P496	Falling Plate cameras	*****	30-35	55-60
P497	Falling Plate cameras (lots)	***	16-20	30-35
P498	Field 1/1 plate	*****	95-100	160-180
> P499	Field 1/2 plate	*****	95-100	160-180
P500	Field 1/4 plate	*****	85-95	150-170
P501	Field 10 * 8 and larger	*****	120-130	200-220
> P502	Folding 6.5 * 9 cm & larger	****	25-30	45-55
P503	Folding plate 4.5 * 6 cm.	****	90-110	160-190
P504	Folding 9 * 12 cm tropical	****	220-260	380-460
P505	Hand & Stand 5*4 (U.S.made)	****	45-50	75-85
P506	Stereo (jumelle type)	****	100-120	180-220
P507	Single Lens Reflex	*****	35-40	60-70
P508	Single Lens Reflex (folding)	****	85-100	140-170
P509	Stereo Field	***	200-240	340-420
P510	Stereo Bellows (wooden)	****	260-300	460-550
P511	Stereo Falling Plate	**	110-130	190-240
P512	Stereo Folding (metal)	****	120-140	200-240
P513	Stereo Wet Plate	***	2200-2700	3900-4800
P514	Strut 6.5 * 9 cm and larger	****	50-60	90-100
P515	Strut 4.5 * 6 cm.	*****	85-95	150-170
P516	Studio with stand	***	130-160	220-260
P517	Studio without stand	****	70-85	120-150
P518	Tailboard 1/1 plate	*****	100-110	170-190
P519	Tailboard 1/2 plate	*****	110-120	190-200
P520	Tailboard 1/4 plate	****	70-85	120-150
P521	Tailboard 10 * 8 and larger	*****	110-120	190-200
P522	Tailboard 9 * 12 cm	**	70-85	120-150
> P523	Tailboard Meagher type	*****	100-110	170-190
P524	Twin Lens Reflex	****	220-260	380-460
P525	Wet Plate (bellows type)	****	200-240	360-420
P526	Wet Plate (sliding box type)	*****	950-1100	1700-1900
Q297	Leica copies	****	70-85	120-150
Q298	S.L.R. (35mm)	****	30-35	50-60

> P499. 1/2 plate Field
... Without doubt the most popular and still the most common of all brass and mahogany cameras made in Britain. In addition to the many makers listed here and elsewhere many thousands were made by small firms and sold direct without names. From c. 1880 onward.

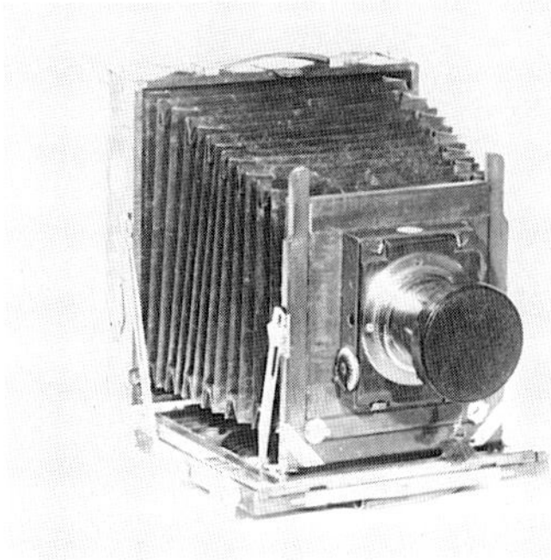

> P502. Folding Cameras
... Folding plate cameras in various sizes both Continental and English became very popular in the 1920's for their relatively small size and quality of results obtainable. Not all have a makers name or type. The 6 * 9 cm was small enough to be pocketable.

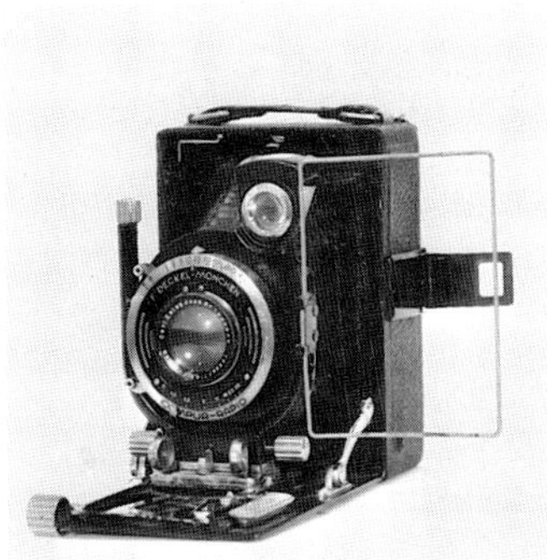

> P523. Meagher Tailboards
... The outriggers which lock the tailboard in position on the camera illustrated were designed by P. Meagher c. 1870. This type of construction was extensively copied so that the term Meagher in due course became generic for all such tailboards.

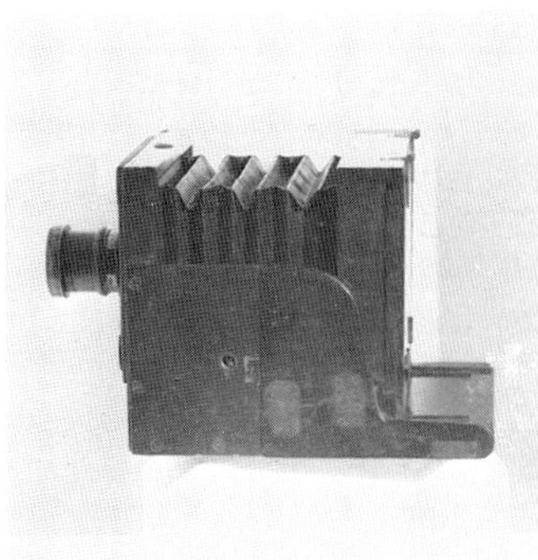

Ref	Name	Data	Average Condition Price Range £	$
Q299	S.L.R. (35mm lots)	**	10-12	17-20
Q300	Viewfinder 35mm (not c.r.f.)	***	15-18	25-30
Q301	Viewfinder 35mm (c.r.f.)	***	25-30	45-55
Q302	Mixed lots of 35mm cameras	*****	9-10	16-18
R460	Rollfilm box coloured (lots)	****	8-10	14-17
R461	Rollfilm box (lots)	*****	5-6	10-11
R462	Rollfilm folding	****	18-20	30-35
R463	Rollfilm folding (lots)	*****	9-10	16-18
R464	Rollfilm V.P.	****	25-30	45-55
R465	Rollfilm V.P.(lots)	***	18-20	30-35
R466	Rollfilm folding with c.r.f	****	30-45	55-80
R467	Rollfilm folding early style	***	40-60	70-100
R468	Rollfilm T.L.R.	****	25-30	45-55
R469	Rollfilm T.L.R. (lots)	****	15-18	25-30
R470	Rollfilm vintage box	***	40-50	70-85
R471	Rollfilm folding coloured	***	25-30	45-55
S72	Automatic table stereoscopes	***	140-170	240-300
S73	Camera lucidas	***	70-85	120-150
> S74	Darkroom lamps	pcc	8-15	13-25
S75	Exposure meters (visual type)	pcc	5-10	9-18
S76	Exposure meters (lots)	***	7-9	13-16
S77	Ferrotype and tintype	***	45-55	80-100
S78	Lenses black-enamelled (lots)	**	7-9	13-16
S79	Lenses brassbound (large)	****	110-130	190-240
S80	Lenses brassbound (lots)	****	12-15	20-25
S81	Magic Lanterns biunnial	***	340-420	600-750
> S82	Magic Lanterns (single wooden)	****	150-170	260-300
S83	Magic Lanterns triunnial	**	2300-2800	4000-4900
S84	Stanhope micro-photo viewers	**	12-15	20-25
S85	Sub-miniature cameras various	***	35-45	65-80
S86	Underwater housings for Leica	**	55-65	95-120
S87	Walking-stick tripods	***	60-75	110-130

> S74. Darkroom Lamps

... One form of collecting photographica is the acquisition of vintage darkroom equipment such as lamps using power sources from candles to paraffin including combination lamps for lighting and printing. Such a collection can be built up at little cost.

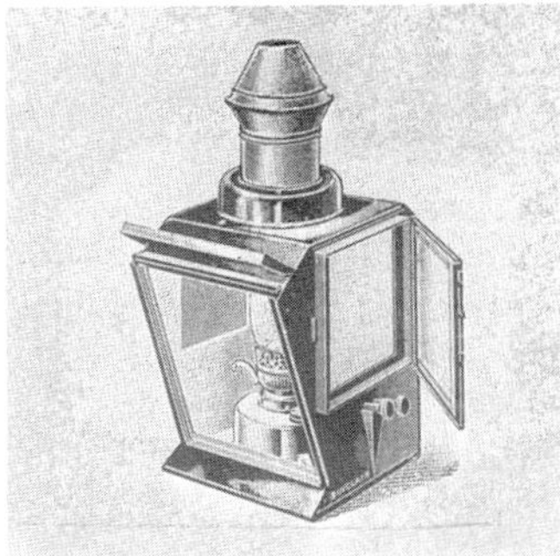

> S82. Magic Lanterns

... These cover a very wide range from tinplate to the elegant triunnial (triple decker) brass and mahogany pieces. With a corresponding price difference of course but all collectable and fun to use. Refs. S81 S82 and S83 cover some different types.

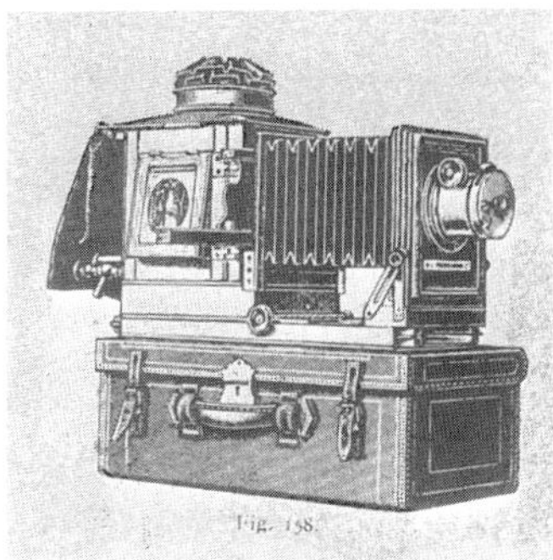

*** AUTHORS and PUBLISHERS NOTE ***

Whilst the opinions expressed in this Pocket Guide are those of the authors their aim has been to provide as much objective and accurate information as practicable to form a basis for the readers own judgement.They believe they have exercised all reasonable care and attention to avoid innaccuracies and mistakes but cannot accept any responsibility for or consequential liability arising from interpretations errors or omissions in the information given.

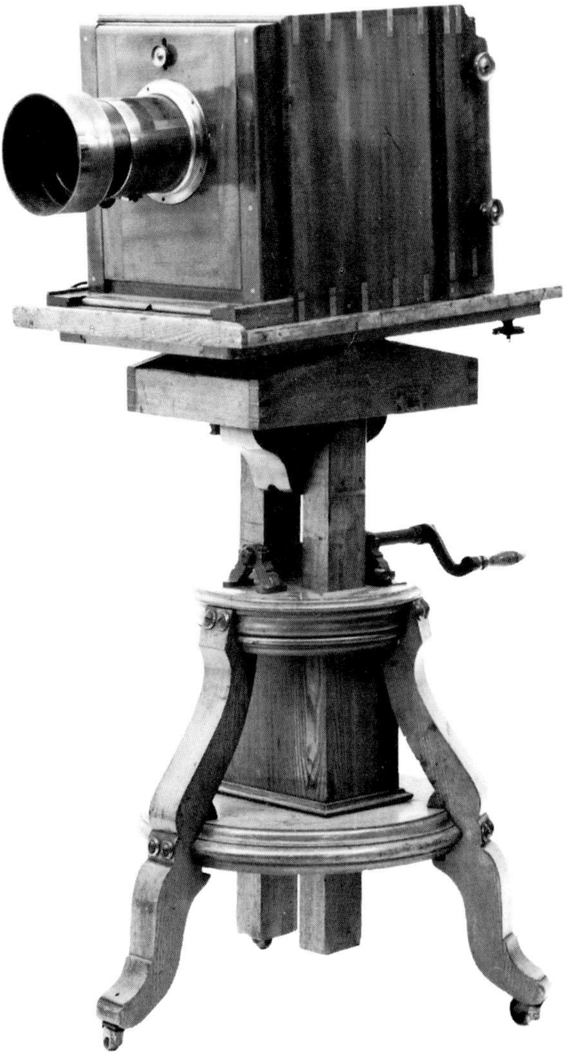